The Hershey, Pennsylvania Cookbook

Fun Treats and Trivia from the Chocolate Capital of the World

Marilyn Odesser-Torpey

ThreeForks™

GUILFORD, CONNECTICUT
HELENA, MONTANA
AN IMPRINT OF THE GLOBE PEQUOT PRESS

Copyright © 2007 Morris Book Publishing, LLC.

ThreeForks is a trademark of Morris Book Publishing, LLC.

CHOCOLATE TOWN USA, GREAT AMERICAN CHOCOLATE BAR, HERSHEY, HERSHEYPARK, HERSHEY'S CHOCOLATE WORLD, HERSHEY'S GREAT AMERICAN CHOCOLATE TOUR, HERSHEY'S KISSES, HERSHEY'S MINI KISSES, HERSHEY'S SPECIAL DARK, KISSES, MOUNDS, REESE'S, SCHARFFEN BERGER, SILVERPOINTS, SWEETEST PLACE ON EARTH, SWEETHEARTS, and YORK are registered trademarks which indicate products of The Hershey Company. LEBBIE LEBKICHER'S, 200 AMERICA, and CHRISTMAS CANDYLANE are trademarks used with permission of Hershey Entertainment & Resorts Company.

Text design by Nancy Freeborn

Photo credits: © Andre Jenny/Alamy: i. Clipart.com: 3, 6, 37, 71. Courtesy of Hershey Community Archives, Hershey, PA: iv (center), vii, x (center), 7, 10, 22 (center), 24, 29, 40 (center), 42, 43 (top right), 45, 69 (center), 87, 102, 104 (center), 112 (center), 124 (center), 129 (center), 132 (center). Courtesy of The Hershey Company: viii. Hershey Entertainment & Resort: 43 (bottom left), 60 (center), 74 (center), 77, 79, 119, 127. Photos.com: iii, iv (back), v, x (back), 1, 5, 13, 17, 20, 22 (back), 23, 30, 33, 40 (back), 41, 43 (back), 49, 52–53, 57–58, 60 (back), 61, 65, 69 (back), 74 (back), 75, 89, 91, 97, 104 (back), 105, 107, 112 (back), 113, 123, 124 (back), 125, 129 (back), 131, 132 (back), 133, 137, 139, 144, 150.

Recipes in this book are courtesy of and reprinted with permission by the following: The Hershey Company (historic recipes and recipes from Hershey's Kitchens). Hershey Entertainment and Resorts (recipes from Hershey Lodge, Hotel Hershey, and Hershey Country Club). Milton Hershey School, Department of School History: pp 33, 34, 49. Hershey-Derry Township Historical Society, www.hersheyhistory.org: pp 26, 39, 135, 140. Other contributors are credited on the recipe pages.

Library of Congress Cataloging-in-Publication Data
Odesser-Torpey, Marilyn.
   The Hershey, Pennsylvania cookbook : fun treats and trivia from the
chocolate capital of the world / Marilyn Odesser-Torpey. — 1st ed.
      p. cm.
   Includes index.
   ISBN 978-0-7627-4155-7
   1. Cookery (Chocolate). 2. Desserts. I. Title.
   TX767.C5043 2007
   641.6'374—dc22
                         2007005468

Manufactured in the United States of America
First Edition/First Printing

contents

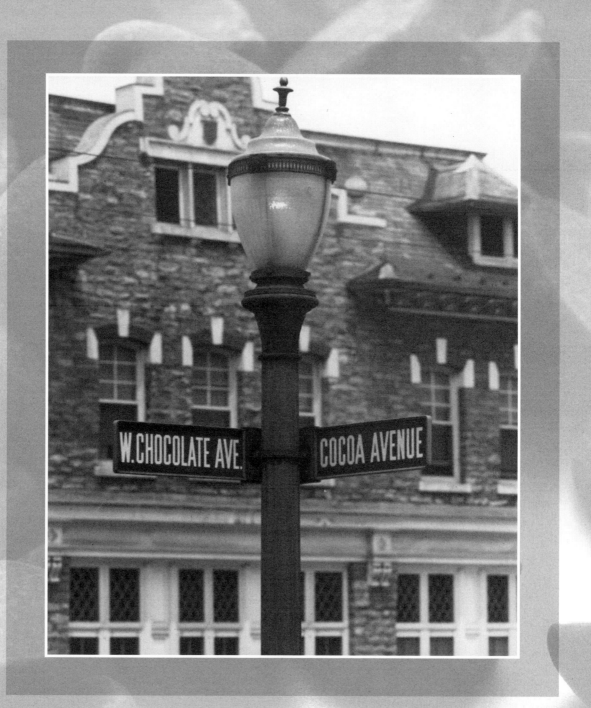

introduction

Chocolate Town USA . . . a Town Built on Chocolate . . . whatever you call it, Hershey, Pennsylvania, sounds like a child's dream come true. And in many ways it is.

Hershey is home to the largest chocolate manufacturing facility in North America. Three factories, including the two-million-square-foot main plant, turn out between three and five million pounds of chocolate each day. The scents wafting from the production lines make Hershey one of the sweetest-smelling towns around.

Every minute 1,500 of the company's milk chocolate bars come off the wrapping line, clad in their familiar brown and silver trade dress. Every day more than eighty million of Hershey's signature Kisses brand chocolates take on their whimsical shapes at plants in Hershey and California. (Hershey also operates confectionery manufacturing plants in nearby Lancaster, Pennsylvania, and in Illinois, Virginia, and Canada.)

With the scent of chocolate teasing your senses, you're not likely to forget the main ingredient that flavors the life of Hershey. But just in case you do, look at the street signs. They bear names like Chocolate and Cocoa Avenues (these two mark the town's main intersection) and the names of tropical locales where cacao beans grow (such as Caracas, Trinidad, Java, Ceylon, and Areba Avenues). Then look at the streetlights, capped with giant Kisses that alternate between "bare chocolate" and "foil-wrapped" versions, the latter sporting Hershey-stamped flags, just like their candy cousins. Even the foliage has sweet things to say, particularly the Chocolate Avenue barberry bushes that are sculpted to spell out HERSHEY COCOA.

> A beautiful town in a valley lay,
> Where a lot of people night and day
> Make Hershey's Chocolate and Cocoa
> As clean and pure as the falling snow . . .
>
> —from Hershey's Green Grass Jingle Book for Little Folks, circa 1915

In the Hotel Hershey—a posh, European-style accommodation built on a hill overlooking the countryside—chocolate bars come with check-in and Kisses chocolates with turndown service. Cacao beans are the key ingredients in spa wraps, baths, and polishes on the menu of the Spa at the Hotel Hershey. Among the signature treatments are Whipped Cocoa Bath (the only thing missing is the marshmallow), Cocoa Massage (classic Swedish-style with chocolate-scented oil), Chocolate Bean Polish (cocoa bean husk and walnut shell exfoliation followed with a slather of cocoa body moisturizer), Chocolate Fondue Wrap (with warmed cocoa-scented mud), and Sweet Hands and Feet (manicure and/or pedicure with a chocolate sugar exfoliation, chocolate mask for the feet, paraffin dip, and massage with chocolate moisturizer).

Soaring into the chocolate-scented sky is a peacock-tail-colored Ferris wheel, the symbol of Hersheypark, a playground with rides and attractions that has been a center of community recreation and entertainment since 1907. For a panoramic of your surroundings, take a ride 250 feet straight up on the Kissing Tower. Safely ensconced in a cozy cabin, you'll view the park through the Hershey Kisses–shaped windows on the rotating ride.

All of these things and more—including a school for children in need, a world-class teaching hospital and medical center, a family-friendly lodge and campground, a twenty-three-acre public garden, and a hometown American Hockey League team—are integral to the past and present of the town that was "built on chocolate." And they are all part of the legacy of one man: Milton Snavely Hershey.

"One of the things I like about this town and like about the company is wherever I traveled, anywhere in the country, when I told people I was from Hershey, they smiled," recalls former marketing department head John H. Dowd, who joined Hershey Chocolate Company in 1966. "I don't imagine people would smile if I said I came from Wilkes-Barre . . . or York or Lancaster. Just the idea of, 'Gee, there's a place called Hershey.' And they smile. It's nice."

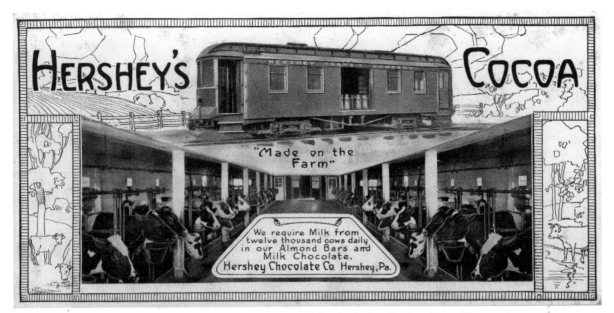

HERSHEY'S COCOA

"Made on the Farm"

We require Milk from twelve thousand cows daily in our Almond Bars and Milk Chocolate. Hershey Chocolate Co. Hershey, Pa.

For many years the promotional cards packaged with Hershey's chocolate bars featured images of the town and company's products. This card was issued between 1909 and 1918.

Born in his great-grandparents' farmhouse about a mile from where his main chocolate factory stands today, Milton Hershey was a complex and colorful character who tried a number of businesses before he hit on chocolate. In the latter part of the nineteenth century, the recipe for making milk chocolate was a well-guarded European secret. Only the extremely well to do could afford to indulge in the velvety sweet.

That is until candy maker Milton Hershey developed his own milk chocolate recipe. His goal was to produce the smooth, creamy chocolate in sufficient volume to be able to offer it to a wider customer base. Toward that end he built a factory in the rural village of Derry Church (often referred to as "the Factory in the Cornfield"), his own hometown in the heart of central Pennsylvania's dairy farmland.

Today the empire that began with a single factory run by the mass-production maestro who has been called "the Henry Ford of Chocolate" reports annual sales of more than $4.4 billion and employs 14,000 people in twenty facilities nationwide. Its products are available in more than ninety countries.

First-time visitors to the area are often surprised to learn that the town of Hershey doesn't really exist—despite the fact that the local post office bears the Hershey name, that between 20,000 and 25,000 residents (6,000 of whom are employed by the chocolate giant) call Hershey home, and that more than four million tourists come every year to sample the town's pleasures. Rather, Hershey is an unincorporated part of Derry Township in Dauphin County, meaning that it has no official boundaries or government of its own. Residents pay their taxes to Derry Township and send their children to its schools.

Of course chocolate is much more than a business in Hershey and surrounding towns. It's a passion that is passed down through generations and permeates traditions from after-school snacks to family picnics to major holidays and other celebrations.

For this book we have combed the historic archives and interviewed families in search of memories, vintage recipes, and photographs that give a flavor of the Hershey of yesteryear. If you

Colorful characters bring the bean-to-bar process to life during the simulated factory tour ride at Hershey's Chocolate World.

have never visited Hershey—or haven't visited for a while—you can "tour" the town as you read this book. Each chapter highlights one of Hershey's main attractions. Town trivia and recipes for treats from current residents and area chefs, bakers, caterers, and bed-and-breakfast owners round out this taste of Hershey today.

To help you replicate these recipes in your home kitchen, we have included chocolate storage and handling hints and baking tips and techniques from Hershey's Kitchens.

And look for the helpful symbols:

 The Kid Friendly icon flags recipes that are simple and fun enough for adults and youngsters to prepare together.

 Hometown Traditions directs you to treats that you're likely to find in family recipe collections and community cookbooks in and around Hershey.

 Vintage Hershey shares Hershey's Kitchens classic recipes from the past.

 Easy Entertaining offers quick-fix recipes to delight your guests.

You'll have to come to Hershey, Pennsylvania, yourself to ride the Kissing Tower or to treat your body to a Chocolate Fondue Wrap, but all you have to do is head for your own kitchen to experience—and share with your family and friends—a taste of how Chocolate Town USA earned the title of Sweetest Place on Earth.

for the love of chocolate

Statistics show that Americans crave chocolate more than any other flavor. More than half (52 percent) of the respondents in a recent survey by the National Confectioners Association named chocolate as their favorite flavor, with berry flavors and vanilla tying for a distant second at 12 percent each.

If not for a couple of twists of fate and an entrepreneurial spirit that was as restless as it was tenacious, this book might well have a very different flavor. Caramel to be exact. It was this golden buttery treat—and not chocolate—that first catapulted central Pennsylvania candy maker Milton Snavely Hershey from struggling entrepreneur to millionaire confectioner.

Actually, the road to success was neither short nor sweet for Milton Hershey, who was born on his paternal grandparents' farm in Derry Township in 1857 to a father, Henry, who had ample imagination but not always adequate funds, and a mother, the former Fannie Snavely, whose down-to-earth values were rooted in her Pennsylvania Dutch Mennonite heritage. That not-always-compatible combination resulted in a family that was often at odds and on the road as Henry launched ventures such as a fruit farm and flower nursery to support his family.

For Milton formal education was an off-and-on-again affair at a number of different schools, finally ending after the fourth grade. At the age of fourteen he went to work, first as an apprentice to the editor of a small-town Pennsylvania newspaper (it is said that he hated the job so much he dropped his straw hat into the printing press to get himself fired), then to a candy maker in the nearby city of Lancaster.

Crisp white uniforms were the order for the day in the 1930s in Hershey's cocoa packaging department.

Four years later, in 1876, eighteen-year-old Milton felt that he was ready for his own entrepreneurial enterprise, a taffy-making shop in Philadelphia. That company lasted for six years, after which Milton traveled to Denver to join his father, who had gone west to seek his fortune in the silver mines. Neither found their fortune in silver, but in the city of Denver, Milton did strike gold, sort of. From a candy maker there, he learned the secret of making meltingly delicious golden caramels using milk instead of the traditional paraffin base.

It took ten more years, three more cities (Chicago, New Orleans, and New York), and another failed business before Hershey was able to turn that gold into personal wealth. Broke, he returned home to Pennsylvania in 1886 at the age of twenty-nine and, on capital borrowed from his mother's sister and a family friend, opened the Lancaster Caramel Company. By 1894 Hershey's "Crystal A" caramel candies had made him one of the wealthiest and most respected businessmen in town.

Some people quote Milton Hershey as saying, "Caramels are only a fad. Chocolate is a permanent thing." Others claim he never uttered those words. Regardless, he became enamored with the cacao bean–based sweet when, during a visit to the 1893 Columbian Exposition in Chicago, he spotted—and purchased—some German-made chocolate-making machinery.

The chocolate that first caught Milton Hershey's fancy in 1893 was not the milk-based confection we now associate with his namesake candy bar. If you've ever tasted a Hershey's Special Dark bar, you'll have a better idea of the bittersweet flavor of the original chocolate recipe.

At first chocolate was just a supporting player in Hershey's company, used to wrap his caramels in an extra robe of flavor, as he had seen done in Europe. But soon the product that had so captured his imagination became the star of his business.

Early additions to his product line included more than one hundred European-style chocolate novelties in a variety of shapes and designs, from simulated cigars to dainty "Princess Wafers," as well as baking chocolate and cocoa. Still elusive for Hershey, however, was the ability to add to his manufacturing repertoire *milk* chocolate, the hand-crafted, silken-textured darling of Europe's moneyed elite since its introduction in Switzerland in 1876.

With characteristic determination Milton Hershey attacked the challenge of developing a cost-efficient formula and the techniques to make the luxury treat affordable for the majority of Americans. In 1900, after several years of experimentation, Hershey's Milk Chocolate Bar made its debut. And at a nickel a bar, Americans ate it up.

Hershey conducted many of his milk-chocolate-making experiments on the Derry Township farm where he had been born. Although the property, now known as "the Homestead," had been sold to pay off creditors in the mid-1860s, Milton Hershey was able to repurchase it in 1897.

Confident that the appetite for his new product would continue to grow, Hershey sold his Lancaster Caramel Company for $1 million that same year to focus on the manufacture of milk chocolate. The "Great American Chocolate Bar" was born, and a great American love affair had begun.

Milton Hershey needed to expand his production capabilities to meet ever-increasing demand. That meant building a larger factory to accommodate sophisticated manufacturing equipment and more employees. Most important of all, it meant finding a plentiful supply of his product's key ingredient—fresh milk.

After exploring other East Coast cities, Hershey found what he needed virtually in his own backyard. In 1905 he moved his entire chocolate-making operation to a brand-new factory built in rural Derry Township, right in the heart of dairy country and close to the very farm on which he had been born.

Titanic Ticket

If Milton S. Hershey had followed his original travel plans on April 10, 1912, he would have been a passenger on the RMS *Titanic* on its maiden—and tragically only—voyage. The chocolatier had put down a deposit to sail on the ship but fortuitously missed the boat due to a "business emergency."

Ninety million pounds of cocoa beans are housed in the Hershey, Pennsylvania, main storage facility, according to the company. That's enough to produce about 5.5 billion milk chocolate bars.

But even the fertile farmlands of Derry couldn't grow the other crucial component in the Hershey candy equation: cacao beans. These come from cacao trees, which have their roots firmly planted in the tropical jungles of South America, Asia, and Africa. The trees bear multiple melonlike fruits called pods. Each pod contains somewhere between twenty and fifty seeds or, as we call them, cocoa beans. According to the National Confectioners Association, it takes about 400 cocoa beans to make one pound of chocolate.

When first harvested the cacao seeds—or beans—are soft. So before they leave their tropical home, they are laid out to dry. During the process, which is called fermentation, the shells harden, the color darkens, and the characteristic cocoa flavor begins to develop.

Different climate and growing conditions impart distinctive flavor elements to the beans. At the Hershey factory, newly arrived beans are sorted by their country of origin. At a later point in the manufacturing process, beans from various countries are combined to create the signature Hershey's blend.

From cocoa bean to finished confection, it takes ten days to make a Hershey's milk chocolate bar. The process begins with a spin in a revolving roaster to develop the deep, rich flavor of the beans. The roasted beans are then shattered to separate the shell from the "nib," the heart of the bean that contains all the flavor.

Only the nibs move on to milling, where they are ground until they release a dark, deeply flavored liquid called "chocolate liquor." (Although it is called "liquor," there is no alcohol in this liquid.) The product we know as "unsweetened" or "baking" chocolate is liquor that has been solidified.

Under hydraulic pressure about half of the vegetable fat, known as cocoa butter, can be extracted from the liquor, leaving the cocoa solids, which are pressed into the form of a cake. When this cake is pulverized, it becomes the unsweetened cocoa powder you find on your store shelves.

Different Ingredients,
Different Personalities

From the basic cacao bean come a number of different types of chocolate. The most common varieties are:

Milk chocolate: At least 10 percent chocolate liquor and at least 12 percent milk or cream are blended with cocoa butter and sugar.

Unsweetened or baking chocolate: This is simply chocolate liquor molded into blocks.

Sweet chocolate: This blend contains cocoa butter, sugar, and at least 15 percent chocolate liquor.

Semisweet or bittersweet chocolate: At least 35 percent chocolate liquor is mixed with cocoa butter and sugar.

White chocolate: Some purists claim that this product shouldn't be classified as chocolate at all because it doesn't contain any nonfat cocoa solids or chocolate liquor. But in 2002 the Food and Drug Administration (FDA) set the white chocolate standard, requiring that it contain at least 20 percent cocoa butter and 14 percent total milk ingredients as well as sugar for flavoring.

It takes approximately
50,000 cows to provide the
700,000 quarts of milk for
one day's production at the
main Hershey, Pennsylva-
nia, chocolate plant.

To make other chocolate products, various quantities of chocolate liquor and cocoa butter are combined with other ingredients, such as sugar and milk, for flavor and texture. (The exception is white chocolate, which contains no chocolate liquor or cocoa powder). The cocoa butter is an important element of eating chocolate: While it is a solid at room temperature, it melts at 89 to 93 degrees Fahrenheit, just below body temperature. That's why chocolate candy melts so luxuriously in your mouth.

Continuing along the milk chocolate production trail, pasteurized fresh milk is mixed with sugar and the resulting combination is slowly dried until it takes on a thick, taffylike consistency. After the precise amount of chocolate liquor is blended in, the mixture is dried into a powder known as "chocolate crumb."

When cocoa butter is added to the crumb and the mixture is ground by steel rollers, the texture gradually becomes smoother until it makes still another transformation into a thick liquid called "chocolate paste." But it's still not the smooth, creamy confection we all know and love.

It takes anywhere from one to three more days of working the chocolate in huge vats, called "conches," with granite rollers to achieve the right texture through a constant motion that's a combination of kneading, grinding, and mixing. The process itself is called "conching."

The last step is tempering, a controlled melting and cooling process that stabilizes the crystals of cocoa butter so the chocolate will have an eye-appealing sheen and a satisfying snap when bitten. During the molding process more than 1,000 bars per minute are formed and are sent on a bumpy ride (vibrations help to remove air bubbles and make sure the chocolate distributes evenly) to the cooling tunnel. Then it's on to packaging.

In the early 1900s employees hand-selected the cocoa beans for Hershey's chocolate products.

Caring for Your Chocolate

Chocolate doesn't ask for much special treatment. Any divalike temperament is tempered out. But if you really love your chocolate, you should store it with care. The Hershey Company recommends keeping your chocolate bars, chips, and chunks in a cool, dry place (65 to 70 degrees Fahrenheit), where it will stay fresh for well over a year. "Bloom," a gray whitish film, may appear on the surface of the chocolate if the temperature varies. Bloom is merely the rising of cocoa butter to the surface and does not affect the quality or taste of the chocolate. Store powdered cocoa at room temperature and avoid contact with moisture and high heat, both of which can cause clumping and gray discoloration. Even if this happens, however, the quality and flavor of the cocoa will not be affected.

Most chocolate confections get their shapes and designs from special molds—but the famous Hershey's Kisses candies do not. Introduced in 1907, Kisses chocolates are simply dropped onto moving steel belts. No one can definitively say how this product got its name, but it has long been speculated that the inspiration was the sound or motion made by the chocolate as it was dropped from the machine to the belt. Actually, say some experts, "kiss" was a common name for a variety of confections before Hershey trademarked the term. (The Hershey Company itself marketed conical-shaped "Sweethearts" seven years before it introduced Kisses and "Silverpoints" eleven years after.)

Until the wrapping process was automated in 1921, each Hershey's Kisses chocolate was wrapped by hand. A small piece of tissue imprinted with the company's name was placed on the inside bottom of each square of foil. Problem was, the name couldn't be read until the candy was unwrapped. To make sure customers knew they were getting the real thing, the Hershey Company developed the idea of leaving a plume of the printed tissue trailing out of the top of each candy, a practice that continues today.

For many years visitors to Hershey, Pennsylvania, could visit the factory and watch chocolate being made. Factory tours stopped in 1972, but the following year Hershey's Chocolate World visitor center opened an entertaining simulation of the process that takes visitors from bean to bar via an interactive ride. Thirty-three years and more than sixty-three million visitors later, the Hershey Company revised the attraction. The tour now features a bull's eye view (with a little mood music provided by a couple of crooning cows) of how Hershey's milk chocolate is made.

(H) chocolate caramels

Combining the two favorite flavors that started it all, this recipe was included in a 1937 booklet entitled *Helps for Hostesses* from the Hershey Chocolate Corporation. Although the recipe doesn't specify what size pan to use, an 8-inch square pan works well.

4 tablespoons butter

1 cup milk

1 cup sugar

1 cup molasses

4 (1-ounce) blocks HERSHEY'S baking chocolate (unsweetened)

2 teaspoons vanilla

1 cup nut meats

1. Place butter in a saucepan; when melted add milk, sugar, and molasses. When the boiling point is reached, add baking chocolate. Boil until a little of the mixture dropped in cold water becomes brittle, then remove from fire.

2. Add vanilla. Beat for 3 minutes. Add nuts; pour at once into the pan. When cold cut into 1-inch squares and wrap in waxed paper.

Makes 64 squares

Instant Chocolate Icing

Why dirty a bowl making frosting for your cookies or cakes? Immediately after baking, simply cover the top surface of the cookie or cake with broken-up pieces of Hershey's milk chocolate bars. Distribute the pieces evenly, then cover loosely with aluminum foil. After approximately five minutes, the chocolate should be soft enough to spread with a knife.

chocolate syrup

Once Hershey's Cocoa Syrup was introduced for commercial use in bakeries, restaurants, and soda fountains in 1926 and for home use two years later, topping ice cream and flavoring milk became as simple as opening a can. Before then, however, cooking up a batch of chocolaty syrup required time and elbow grease. Published in the *1990 Betty Groff's Pennsylvania Dutch Cookbook* by central Pennsylvania food authority Betty Groff, this recipe was featured for years at an ice-cream shop in Hershey and given to Groff by former Hershey corporate president James E. Bobb.

1 cup HERSHEY'S unsweetened cocoa

4 cups (2 pounds) sugar

1 teaspoon salt

6 cups water

2 tablespoons arrowroot, dissolved in
   ¼ cup water

1 tablespoon vanilla

1. Sift the cocoa, sugar, and salt. Put into a 5-quart pan and gradually whisk in the water over medium heat. Bring to a boil, stirring constantly.

2. As it comes to a boil, mix in the arrowroot and cook for 5 minutes, until thickened. Remove from heat and stir in vanilla.

3. Store in airtight jars and refrigerate.

   Makes 1½ quarts

Hershey's Fountain Cocoa packaging from the years 1910 to 1925.

10 POUNDS   NET WEIGHT

Hershey's

FOUNTAIN COCOA

ABSOLUTELY PURE

PREPARED ONLY BY THE

HERSHEY CHOCOLATE CO.

HERSHEY, PA. U.S.A.

soft pan brownies

Where there's chocolate, there are all kinds of brownie recipes. And every baker swears that the one he or she has is the absolute best. For example, Kathy Burrows, who grew up in Hershey and works for Hershey Entertainment & Resorts, swears by a recipe she found in the 1972 *Bountiful Harvest Cookbook* published by the Palmyra Church of the Brethren. (Palmyra is a small town right outside of Hershey.) Originally submitted to the book by church member Ann Groff, these brownies don't contain baking powder so they're very dense.

Kathy Burrows still saves every shoebox she can find to fill with these brownies and mail to her grown sons and other family members and friends who constantly request them. Through the years boxes of these homemade bars have even made their way to soldiers in the Middle and Far East.

$1/3$ cup Crisco or other vegetable shortening

4 tablespoons butter

4 tablespoons cocoa

2 eggs

1 cup sugar

$1/2$ teaspoon vanilla

$3/4$ cup flour

$1/4$ teaspoon salt

$3/4$ cup chopped nuts

1. Melt shortening and butter; add cocoa and stir until well blended. Cool.

2. Beat eggs in a small mixing bowl. Add sugar and vanilla; beat well. Add cocoa mixture to eggs and sugar; mix well. Add flour, salt, and nuts; mix well. Spread evenly in a greased 8-inch pan; bake at 325°F for 25 minutes.

3. To make icing: Place unwrapped chocolate bars on top of brownies immediately after taking the pan from the oven. Spread the chocolate over the brownies. Let cool; cut into squares.

Serves 9 to 12

CHEF NOTE: In the original recipe, Ann Groff used melted chocolate bars for her brownie icing. She doesn't specify how many, but four or five should do it. Kathy, on the other hand, often skips the icing altogether and just stirs a cup of chocolate chips right into the unbaked batter for a similar, superfudgey effect. She does the same thing with broken up pieces of Reese's peanut butter cups or York peppermint patties. (You can also use Hershey's Premier Baking Pieces, which are tiny chocolate pieces filled with caramel, or Reese's Premier Baking Pieces, which are just like the original peanut butter cups.)

"tasty" peanut butter and chocolate bars

With their moist, tender, golden cake, creamy peanut butter filling, and tooth-satisfying bite of candy bar "frosting," these snack squares are reminiscent of a treat that's been a longtime Philadelphia favorite. When the melted Hershey's milk chocolate bars spread on top cool in the refrigerator, the chocolate regains its pleasing "snap." This recipe is attributed to Pauline Greiner in the 1992 *Ladies of the Church* cookbook published by the Trinity Evangelical Lutheran Church in Colebrook, a community only a few miles outside of Hershey, Pennsylvania.

4 eggs

1/8 teaspoon salt

2 cups sugar

1 cup milk

1 teaspoon vanilla

2 teaspoons baking powder

2 cups flour

2 teaspoons margarine or butter, softened

1 small jar peanut butter

2 (8-ounce) HERSHEY bars

1. In a large bowl combine the cake ingredients (eggs, salt, sugar, milk, vanilla, baking powder, flour, and margarine or butter) and mix well until smooth. Pour onto a greased and floured cookie sheet. Bake at 350°F for 20 minutes.

2. While cake is still warm, spread peanut butter over top until the entire cake is covered. Set aside in the refrigerator for at least 1 hour or until peanut butter is hard.

3. Melt the chocolate bars in the top of a double boiler over hot water. While still warm, spread melted chocolate over peanut butter layer. Refrigerate for several more hours, preferably overnight, until chocolate is set. Cut into squares.

Serves 16

Cooking with Chocolate

Many recipes call for melted chocolate. Whether you're melting bars or chips, keep in mind that water is chocolate's worst enemy. According to the Hershey Company and other chocolate experts, any amount of moisture—from humidity in the air to a couple of drops of water on your spoon to the steam or condensation rising from the bottom of your double boiler—can cause chocolate to stiffen up and take on a grainy texture. This is called "seizing."

If seizing should occur, you can stir in a very small amount of solid vegetable shortening (one level tablespoon for each six ounces of chocolate). Do not ever use butter, margarine, spreads, oil, water, or milk.

Keep a close eye on the temperature, because chocolate can scorch easily. It also helps to stir the chocolate periodically during the melting process. If you are using the microwave for melting, don't rely on your eye to tell you when the chocolate's ready. Baking chips and other chocolate products may maintain their form and appear to be solid until you stir them. Since all microwaves are different, follow the manufacturer's instructions for your specific make and model.

A scorch-proof melting method is to place the chips or broken chocolate pieces in a small, heat-safe bowl or cup, then place the container in a shallow pan that contains a small amount of water (not too much or you might splash). Let the bowl sit for a few minutes and stir the chocolate periodically until it is smooth.

Hershey bar pie

Proof of the wide appeal of Hershey's milk chocolate is this recipe that comes all the way from the Lone Star State. Whether or not this creamy pie originated in Pennsylvania isn't certain—but this version, published in the 1976 *Dallas Junior League Cookbook,* found its way back to Hershey and into the favorites file of Susan Fowler, executive director of the Hershey Theatre.

1 cup crushed graham crackers

$\frac{1}{2}$ cup coconut

$\frac{1}{3}$ cup melted butter

$\frac{1}{4}$ cup confectioners' sugar

2 teaspoons instant coffee

2 tablespoons hot water

7$\frac{1}{2}$ ounces HERSHEY'S milk chocolate bar with almonds

1 (8-ounce) container Cool Whip

1 tablespoon rum (optional)

1. To make crust: Combine graham crackers, coconut, melted butter, and confectioners' sugar. Press into a 9-inch pie pan and bake at 350°F for 10 minutes. Cool.

2. To make filling: Dissolve coffee in 2 tablespoons hot water in a saucepan. Melt Hershey bars in coffee mixture over low heat. Remove coffee/chocolate mixture from heat and add Cool Whip and rum. Pour into crust and freeze until firm.

Serves 8

(H) Hershey's bar or Kisses pie with chocolate petal crust

This second variation of the Hershey Bar Pie made its original debut in a 1975 recipe brochure for Hershey's cocoa; the recipe has since been updated by Hershey's Kitchen. This one's particularly easy and perfect for first-time pie bakers. Instead of rolling out a regular piecrust dough, you cut the dough like slice-and-bake cookies and arrange the slices one by one on the pan to create the Chocolate Petal Crust.

1/2 cup butter or margarine

1 cup sugar

1 egg

1 teaspoon vanilla

1 1/4 cups flour

1/2 cup HERSHEY'S unsweetened cocoa

3/4 teaspoon baking soda

1/4 teaspoon salt

5 (1.05-ounce) bars HERSHEY'S milk chocolate with almonds or 1 1/3 cups (8 ounces) HERSHEY'S MINI KISSES milk chocolates

1/3 cup milk

1 1/2 cups miniature or 15 large marshmallows

1 cup (1/2 pint) whipping cream

sweetened whipping cream and additional MINI KISSES chocolates for decoration

1. To make the Chocolate Petal Crust: Beat butter, sugar, egg, and vanilla in a large bowl until fluffy. Stir together flour, cocoa, baking soda, and salt; beat into butter mixture. Shape soft dough into two rolls about 7 1/2 inches long. Wrap each roll in waxed paper or plastic wrap (dough will be soft); refrigerate several hours or overnight.

2. Preheat oven to 375°F. Grease a 9-inch pie plate. Cut one roll into 1/8-inch-thick slices. Place the slices, edges touching, on bottom and up side of prepared pie plate. (Spaces between slices of dough in crust fill in during baking.) Bake for 8 to 10 minutes. Cool completely before filling. (Makes enough dough for 2 crusts.)

3. To make filling: Chop chocolate bars into small pieces. In the top of a double boiler, melt chocolate with milk over hot—not boiling—water. Or microwave chocolate pieces with milk in large microwave-safe bowl at high (100% power) for 1 minute; stir until well blended. Cool to room temperature. Stir in marshmallows. Microwave 30 seconds; stir. If necessary, microwave an additional 15 seconds at a time, stirring after each heating until marshmallows are melted. Cool to room temperature.

4. Beat whipping cream in a medium bowl until stiff; carefully fold into chocolate mixture. Spoon into prepared crust. Refrigerate until firm, about 4 hours. Garnish with sweetened whipped cream and chocolate pieces. Cover; refrigerate leftover pie.

Serves 8

CHEF NOTE: This recipe yields 2 piecrusts. The remaining roll of dough may be frozen up to 6 weeks for later use.

cocoa surprise cookies

cocoa surprise cookies Mary Eckert, a member of the Trinity Evangelical Lutheran Church in Colebrook, Pennsylvania, made these family favorites doubly delightful by tucking two surprises—bits of caramel and marshmallow—into each cookie. Here is Mary Eckert's recipe as it originally appeared in her congregation's 1992 cookbook, *Ladies of the Church*.

2 eggs

1⅓ cups butter-flavored shortening

2 teaspoons vanilla

1 cup sugar

⅔ cup packed brown sugar

2¼ cups flour

⅔ cup HERSHEY'S unsweetened cocoa

1¼ teaspoons baking soda

9 marshmallows, cut into quarters
   (or 36 miniature marshmallows)

9 bite-site square caramels, cut into
   quarters

1. Beat eggs, shortening, vanilla, and sugars. Add flour, cocoa, and baking soda. Mix well. Chill mixture in a large bowl, covered, at least 1 hour.

2. Roll dough, 1 tablespoon at a time, into balls. Make an indentation in each ball and place 1 caramel quarter and 1 marshmallow quarter (or miniature marshmallow) inside. Roll ball to close the indentation, making sure the caramel and marshmallow are completely covered.

3. Place balls on ungreased cookie sheets, 6 balls per sheet. Bake at 350°F for 10 minutes or until set. Allow cookies to cool for 3 to 4 minutes before transferring them to wire racks. Store in airtight containers.

Makes 2½ to 3 dozen

forgotten Kisses cookies

Light, airy, and meltingly good, these meringue cookies from the test kitchens at Hershey contain no flour, egg yolks, or shortening. The Hershey's Kisses chocolate maintains its signature shape when the cookies are done.

2 egg whites

1/8 teaspoon cream of tartar

1/8 teaspoon salt

2/3 cup sugar

1 teaspoon vanilla

36 HERSHEY'S KISSES chocolates, unwrapped

1. Preheat oven to 375°F. Grease a cookie sheet. In a small bowl, beat egg whites with cream of tartar and salt until soft peaks form. Gradually beat in sugar, 1 tablespoon at a time; continue beating until stiff peaks form, mixture is glossy, and sugar is dissolved. Stir in vanilla.

2. Drop meringue by 1/2 teaspoonfuls onto the prepared cookie sheet; top with chocolate piece. Cover chocolate with a small teaspoonful of meringue, making certain to completely cover chocolate. Place cookies in hot oven, then turn off oven and allow cookies to remain overnight or until oven has cooled completely.

Makes about 30 cookies

CHEF NOTE: Omit the Hershey's Kisses and substitute 1 cup Hershey's semisweet or milk chocolate chips. Fold the chips into the meringue and drop by teaspoonful onto a greased baking sheet. Baked as the original recipe directs. This variation makes about 3 dozen cookies.

mudslide cookies

Three different varieties of chocolate make these cookies served at the Cocoa Beanery restaurant in the Hershey Lodge ultrarich, dense, and ultrachocolaty. If you really want to make guests swoon, serve the cookies warm from the oven or pop them in the microwave for a couple of seconds before serving.

flourless cooking spray for greasing pan

$3/4$ cup plus 2 tablespoons cake flour

1 tablespoon baking powder

$1/8$ teaspoon salt

1 tablespoon instant coffee powder

1 tablespoon boiling water

1 teaspoon vanilla

7 ounces HERSHEY'S unsweetened chocolate, coarsely chopped

6 ounces HERSHEY'S semisweet chocolate, coarsely chopped

8 tablespoons unsalted butter

7 large eggs

$2 3/4$ cups sugar

2 cups chopped walnuts

$1 1/2$ cups HERSHEY'S semisweet chocolate chips

1. Preheat oven to 350°F. Lightly spray cookie sheets or line them with parchment. Sift flour, baking powder, and salt into a bowl and set aside.

2. Combine the instant coffee and boiling water to make a paste; blend in vanilla.

3. Melt the chopped unsweetened and semisweet chocolates along with the butter in a saucepan over medium low heat or in the microwave in 15- to 20-second intervals; gently stir to blend.

4. In an electric mixer fitted with a whisk attachment, beat together the eggs, sugar, and coffee paste mixture on high speed until light in texture and thick, 6 to 8 minutes. Add the chocolate mixture with the machine running on medium speed. On low speed, mix in the dry ingredients until just blended. Mix in the walnuts and chocolate chips until blended. Scrape down the bowl as needed during mixing to blend evenly.

5. Using a $1/4$-cup measure as a scoop, fill it with dough, level it, and drop dough onto the prepared cookie sheet, leaving 3 to 4 inches between the cookies. Bake until cookies are cracked on top but still slightly moist, rotating the pans as necessary to bake evenly, 14 minutes. Allow cookies to cool slightly on the sheet before transferring them to wire racks to cool completely.

Makes 24 cookies

A Bite of History

Who says making party food was hard labor before the invention of food processors and other later twentieth-century modern appliances? According to *Hershey's Helps for the Hostess* published by the Hershey Chocolate Company in 1934, "'Toasted Chocolate Sandwiches' are a novelty which the hostess can utilize for many occasions. They are ideal for the after-theatre or after-the-game supper or snack, or for any informal party or gathering. Hershey's Milk Chocolate or Hershey's Almond Bar is the chief ingredient of these delicious treats. They may be prepared from different kinds of bread, cake, or crackers, with the addition of other unusual and tempting tidbits." Note the price of the candy bar specified by the original recipe!

Toasted Chocolate Sandwiches

1 tablespoon butter

2 thin slices white bread

1 "five-cent" HERSHEY'S milk chocolate bar

1. Leave crusts on bread. Place milk chocolate between 2 slices of bread, sandwich fashion, using enough of the bar to neatly cover the bread.

2. Melt butter in a skillet and lay in sandwich. When bottom slice is brown, turn carefully over with spatula; brown reverse side. Serve immediately.

VARIATIONS: Alaska Toasted Sandwich—Butter 2 slices of thinly cut angel cake. Lay milk chocolate bar between slices, sandwich fashion. Toast in electric toaster. Chocolate Marmalade Sandwich—Butter 2 slices thinly cut sponge cake. Spread inside with orange marmalade. Lay milk chocolate bar between slices, sandwich fashion. Toast in electric toaster.

triple chocolate cherry truffle squares

Each year county fairs throughout Pennsylvania hold Hershey's Cocoa Classic Chocolate Cake, Cookie, Brownie, and Bar Baking Contests. First-place winners are entered in the statewide competition at the annual Pennsylvania Farm Show held in the capital city of Harrisburg. Festive red cherries peek through the tops of these three-layer bars that earned Pennsylvania resident John Neidlinger second place in the state farm show's Hershey's Cookie/Brownie/Bar category in 2004. The squares are very rich, so you'll probably want to cut them small.

....

$^1/_2$ **cup sugar**

$^1/_4$ **cup shortening**

$^1/_4$ **cup butter, softened**

$^1/_4$ **teaspoon vanilla**

$^1/_4$ **teaspoon almond extract**

1 egg

1 cup all-purpose flour

$^1/_4$ **teaspoon baking soda**

$^1/_4$ **teaspoon cream of tartar**

$^1/_3$ **cup HERSHEY'S semisweet chocolate chips**

$^1/_4$ **cup butter**

$^1/_4$ **cup HERSHEY'S unsweetened cocoa**

3 tablespoons light corn syrup

1 tablespoon milk

2 cups confectioners' sugar

1 (10-ounce) jar maraschino cherries, drained and chopped

1 cup HERSHEY'S Premier White Chips

2 tablespoons shortening

milk chocolate shavings (for garnish)

1. To make the crust: Preheat oven to 350°F. In a mixing bowl, combine sugar, $^1/_4$ cup shortening, and $^1/_4$ cup softened butter; beat until light and fluffy. Add vanilla, almond extract, and egg; beat well. Add flour, baking soda, and cream of tartar; mix well. Spread evenly into a greased 9 x 13 x 2-inch pan. Bake for about 11 minutes or until golden brown. Set aside 45 minutes to cool.

2. To make the filling: In a medium microwave-safe bowl, combine chocolate chips and $^1/_4$ cup butter. Microwave on high for 1 or 2 minutes, stirring every 30 seconds until melted and smooth. Add cocoa, corn syrup, and milk; blend well. Add confectioners' sugar and mix until smooth and spreadable. If the mixture is too stiff to spread, add a little more milk a couple of drops at a time. Spread mixture over cooled crust. Top with cherries; gently press into filling.

3. To make the topping: In a small microwave-safe bowl, combine white chips and 2 tablespoons shortening. Microwave on high for 30 seconds; stir. Continue microwaving, stirring every 10 seconds, until chips are melted and stirred smooth. (If the chips and shortening mixture is too stiff to spread, add a little bit more shortening.)

4. Spoon topping over filling. Refrigerate 20 minutes until set. Top with chocolate shavings. Cut into squares when ready to serve.

Makes 36 bars

family traditions

His friends thought that the Derry Township farm-country site Milton Hershey had chosen for his new chocolate factory was "too remote." His own wife suggested that he "have his head examined," according to company historic literature. But Hershey had done some extensive site—and soul—searching and determined that his old hometown could provide everything he needed to build a solid foundation for his growing company.

Of course, there was the milk, a virtually endless supply produced fresh every day on surrounding farms. The area also provided plentiful quantities of clean water and access to the nearby ports of Philadelphia and New York, vital sources of essential ingredients, such as cocoa beans and sugar, that could not be produced in Derry. Just as important, the area offered a large potential workforce of Pennsylvania Dutch (the name is a variation on the word "Deutsch," referring to the Germans and Swiss Germans), like his own family, and Scots-Irish. Local limestone and brownstone quarries had also attracted a number of Italian stonecutters, who had brought their families along with them in their quest for employment and settled here when they found it.

In 1903 Milton Hershey broke ground for his new factory about 1 mile from the family homestead on which he was born. Chocolate production began in 1905 in facilities that *Confectioners' Journal* described as "the most complete of their kind in the world," according to the Hershey-Derry Township Historical Society.

> "Be sorry for people whoever they are, Who live in a house where there's no cookie jar!"
> —from an undated issue of Hershey's Kitchens' *Chocolate Town Bulletin*

Milton S. and Catherine Hershey.

A Peek into the Past

If you want to learn more about the native and immigrant groups that provided the historic and cultural foundations for Derry Township and the town called Hershey, visit the Hershey Museum. Opened in 1933, this museum houses Milton Hershey's personal collections of Native American and Pennsylvania German ("Deutsch") objects and artifacts as well as display items and interactive exhibits dedicated to the founding and growth of the corporate giant and "the Town Built on Chocolate." Two other great resources for Hershey history are the Hershey Community Archives and the Hershey-Derry Township Historical Society.

From little Derry Township, Hershey's milk chocolate would become the first nationally marketed product of its kind. Because he had no predecessors in this area, Hershey either created or adapted most of the mass-production machinery for his factory.

But his goal was to build more than a business. Hershey wanted to build a town and, more than that, a model town that workers would be happy to call home. So Hershey authorized the construction of worker houses, and then he had a trolley system built so that workers living in neighboring communities could easily make the commute.

A view of Chocolate Avenue circa 1920 to 1925.

Milton and Catherine Hershey had their own home built on a rise overlooking the factory. They lived in that home, which they called High Point, until Catherine's death in 1915. In 1930 Milton donated High Point to the Hershey Country Club to serve as its member clubhouse.

The Great Depression didn't deter Milton Hershey from fulfilling his promise to the families who had become the foundation of the town. While the rest of the nation suffered from staggeringly high levels of unemployment as business after business succumbed to the hard economic times of the 1930s, the town of Hershey prospered and grew. To keep his people working, Hershey initiated a "Great Building Campaign," during which such landmark structures as the Hotel Hershey and the Hershey Theatre were constructed.

In a film celebrating the town's centennial, historians compared the influx of job seekers into Hershey during the Depression era to the swelling of the towns in the American West during the gold rush less than a century earlier. More than 600 men who may well have found themselves unemployed during the Depression were able to support themselves and their families by working on Hershey's Great Building Campaign.

Moving Experience

In her Hershey Community Archives oral history, Madeline Hite recalled how she learned that her family was about to move to Hershey in 1934. "My father came home with a pocketful of Kisses," she said. "And I thought, 'This is the place for me!' "

Uncommon Community

Milton Hershey wasn't terribly happy that the first homes built in his new town all looked alike. Although the houses were charming and comfortable, he thought the sameness of the design gave the community the look of a mass-manufactured factory town. Hershey subsequently required his builders to use a wide variety of styles and designs. In the early days one could rent a house in Hershey for $10 a month or own one for $1,200. Individuals were welcome to buy lots and build their own homes, but there were some basic rules: "no taverns; piggeries; soap, candle or blacksmith shops" could be located in the residential areas, according to Hershey-Derry Township Historical Society records.

chocolate-almond biscotti

Residents of Hershey, Pennsylvania, have always found delectable ways to keep their cookie jars filled. This satisfyingly crunchy two-tone treat, from local resident and member of the Hershey-Derry Township Historical Society Joanne Lewis Curry, reflects the town's Italian heritage. The recipe appears in the society's 2003 *Hershey Centennial Cookbook*.

1/2 cup butter or margarine, softened

1 1/4 cups sugar

2 eggs

1 teaspoon almond extract

2 1/4 cups flour

1/4 cup HERSHEY'S unsweetened cocoa

1 teaspoon baking powder

1/4 teaspoon salt

1 cup sliced almonds

1 cup HERSHEY'S semisweet chocolate chips

1 tablespoon shortening (do not use butter, margarine, spread, or oil)

1/4 cup white chocolate chips

1 teaspoon shortening (do not use butter, margarine, spread, or oil)

1. Preheat oven to 350°F. Beat butter and sugar in a large bowl until well blended. Add eggs and almond extract; beat until smooth.

2. Stir together flour, cocoa, baking powder, and salt. Gradually add to butter mixture, beating until smooth. (Dough will be thick.) Stir in almonds with wooden spoon.

3. Divide dough in half. With lightly floured hands, shape each half into a rectangular log about 2 inches in diameter and 11 inches long; place at least 2 inches apart on a large ungreased cookie sheet. Bake for 30 minutes or until logs are set. Remove from oven; cool on cookie sheet for 15 minutes. Using a serrated knife in a sawing motion, cut logs diagonally into 1/2-inch thick slices. Discard end pieces. Arrange slices, cut sides down, close together on cookie sheet; bake for 8 to 9 minutes. Turn slices over; bake an additional 8 or 9 minutes. Remove from oven; cool on cookie sheet on wire rack.

4. To make the chocolate glaze: Place semisweet chocolate chips and 1 tablespoon shortening in a small microwave-safe dish; microwave on high (100% power) for 1 to 1 1/2 minutes or until smooth when stirred (makes about 1 cup).

5. To make the white glaze: Place white chocolate chips and 1 teaspoon shortening in a small microwave-safe dish; microwave on high (100% power) for 30 to 45 seconds or until smooth when stirred (makes 1/4 cup).

6. Dip end of each biscotti in chocolate glaze or drizzle glaze over entire cookie. Drizzle white glaze over chocolate glaze. Garnish with additional almonds, if desired.

Makes 2 1/2 dozen cookies

"wicked" whoopie pies

Not really pies at all, but two moist, tender cake shells sandwiching a hearty helping of fluffy white frosting, these treats are often attributed to the Pennsylvania Dutch and are, indeed, a staple found in just about every bakery, grocery store, and community cookbook in the south-central part of the state. However, many food historians believe that these stuffed sweets originated in New England.

Some of the best whoopies I've ever tasted are made by Isamax Snacks (under the name Wicked Whoopies) in Gardiner, Maine. Isamax founder and owner Amy Bouchard has graciously shared the recipe for her award-winning whoopies, which Oprah Winfrey chose as a "great gift" in 2003 on her television program and, once again, in 2004 on her Web site. Why are they called whoopie pies? No one really knows. But they do make people happy!

4 heaping cups sifted flour

2 teaspoons salt

2 teaspoons baking soda

$\frac{1}{2}$ cup shortening

$\frac{1}{2}$ cup butter

2 cups sugar

2 eggs

1 teaspoon vanilla

1 cup sour milk (or 1 tablespoon vinegar and enough milk to make 1 cup)

1 cup cocoa

1 cup hot water

6 tablespoons marshmallow crème

4 tablespoons vanilla

4 tablespoons flour

4 tablespoons milk

4 cups confectioners' sugar

$1\frac{1}{2}$ cups shortening

1. Sift together 4 cups sifted flour, salt, and baking soda and set aside.

2. Mix together $\frac{1}{2}$ cup shortening, butter, 2 cups sugar, eggs, and vanilla. Add sour milk, cocoa, and hot water. Add dry ingredients.

3. Scoop large rounded spoonfuls of batter onto a greased cookie sheet, space at least 2 inches apart. Bake at 350°F for 10 minutes. Let cakes cool completely.

4. To make filling, combine marshmallow crème, vanilla, 4 tablespoons flour, 4 tablespoons milk, 4 cups confectioners' sugar, and $1\frac{1}{2}$ cups shortening in a bowl and beat until smooth. Scoop 1 large rounded tablespoon of the filling between the cake shells.

Makes about 2 dozen pies

funny pie

Shoofly pie is a Pennsylvania Dutch specialty dessert that marries a sweet, gooey base of molasses with a baked-on cakelike crumb topping. Betty Groff, who lives in Mount Joy, Pennsylvania, fewer than 20 miles from Hershey, got this chocolate version from a friend in Cincinnati and featured it in her 1987 *Betty Groff's Country Goodness Cookbook.*

1 cup sugar

$\frac{1}{2}$ teaspoon salt

$\frac{1}{2}$ cup unsweetened cocoa

$\frac{3}{4}$ cup hot water

1 teaspoon vanilla

$\frac{1}{2}$ cup butter, at room temperature

2 cups sugar

2 eggs

2 cups flour

$\frac{1}{2}$ teaspoon salt

2 teaspoons baking powder

1 cup milk

$\frac{3}{4}$ teaspoon vanilla

2 unbaked 9-inch pie shells

1. To make the liquid pie bottom: Stir 1 cup sugar, $\frac{1}{2}$ teaspoon salt, and unsweetened cocoa together in a saucepan. Slowly add the hot water and blend until smooth. Bring to a boil and simmer for 5 minutes. Remove from the heat and add 1 teaspoon vanilla. Cool while preparing batter for topping.

2. For the topping: Cream the butter and 2 cups sugar in mixing bowl. Beat in the eggs, 1 at a time. Sift the flour, $\frac{1}{2}$ teaspoon salt, and baking powder into another bowl. Gradually beat into the butter-sugar-egg mixture, alternately with the milk, until smooth. Add the vanilla.

3. Pour the cooled liquid bottom mixture into the unbaked pie shells. Drop the topping batter evenly over the liquid bottom. Bake in a preheated 375°F oven for 50 to 60 minutes until filling is firm when pan is moved.

Makes 2 (9-inch) pies

Kisses from Mom

Milton Hershey "had a wonderful mother. I never met her, but I knew about her," said Ruth Boyer in her Hershey Community Archives oral history. So did just about everyone else who worked in the chocolate factory in the days before packaging automation. Many remember Milton Hershey's mother, Fanny, taking trays of Kisses chocolates home to wrap by hand.

chocolate pecan pie

Add chocolate to the ooey-gooey goodness of pecan pie and you have a slice of something that goes beyond heavenly. This recipe is from the Hershey Lodge. If you want to gussy it up a bit for company, you can top each slice with sweetened whipped cream or vanilla ice cream.

1 cup sugar

1/3 cup **HERSHEY'S** unsweetened cocoa

3 eggs, slightly beaten

3/4 cup light corn syrup

1 tablespoon butter or margarine, melted

1 teaspoon vanilla

1 cup pecan halves

1 unbaked 9-inch piecrust

1. Preheat oven to 350°F. Stir together sugar and cocoa in a medium bowl. Add eggs, corn syrup, butter, and vanilla; stir until well blended. Stir in pecans.

2. Pour into unbaked piecrust. Bake for 60 minutes or until set. Remove from oven to wire rack. Cool completely.

Makes 1 (9-inch) pie

Early Earnings

Mary Bonawitz recalls that in 1934, when she was eighteen years old, she stood outside the Hershey Chocolate Factory for three days hoping to be chosen for employment. In her oral history in the Hershey Community Archives, she tells of beginning on the Kisses belt, picking out defective candies, then moving on to the molding room, where she worked for thirty-two years. When she received her first paycheck of thirty-two dollars (thirty-two cents an hour), "I felt rich," she remembers. The next year her hourly rate was raised to thirty-seven cents.

chocolate cookie pretzels

Pretzels are a major part of the food heritage of the Pennsylvania Dutch. Usually they are savory treats made of yeasted dough topped with a generous sprinkling of coarse salt. This interpretation gives the pretzel a distinctly Hershey's twist. It should since it comes from the candy company's test kitchen.

$^2/_3$ **cup butter or margarine, softened**

1 cup sugar

2 teaspoons vanilla

2 eggs

2$^1/_2$ cups all-purpose flour

$^1/_2$ cup HERSHEY'S unsweetened cocoa

$^1/_2$ teaspoon baking soda

$^1/_4$ teaspoon salt

confectioner's sugar or Satiny Chocolate Glaze or Peanut Butter Chip Frosting (optional; see page 31)

1. Preheat oven to 350°F. Beat butter, sugar, and vanilla in a large bowl until fluffy. Add eggs; beat well. Stir together flour, cocoa, baking soda, and salt; gradually add to butter mixture, beating until well blended.

2. Divide dough into 24 pieces. On a lightly floured surface, roll each piece with hands into a pencil-like strip about 12 inches long. Place strip on ungreased cookie sheet. Twist into pretzel shape by crossing left side of strip to middle, forming loop. Fold right side up and over first loop. Place about 2 inches apart on cookie sheet.

3. Bake for 8 minutes or until set. Cool 1 minute; remove from cookie sheet to wire rack. Cool completely. Sprinkle with confectioners' sugar, if desired, or frost.

Makes 2 dozen cookies

satiny chocolate glaze

2 tablespoons butter or margarine

3 tablespoons HERSHEY'S unsweetened cocoa

2 tablespoons water

1/2 teaspoon vanilla

1 cup confectioners' sugar

1. Melt butter in a small saucepan over low heat; add cocoa and water. Cook, stirring constantly, until mixture thickens; do not boil. Remove from heat; stir in vanilla. Gradually add confectioners' sugar, beating with whisk until smooth. Add additional water, 1/2 teaspoon at a time, until glaze is of desired consistency.

Makes about 3/4 cup

peanut butter chip frosting

1 cup confectioners' sugar

1/4 cup (1/2 stick) butter or margarine

3 tablespoons milk

1 cup REESE'S peanut butter chips

1/2 teaspoon vanilla

1. Measure confectioners' sugar into a medium bowl; set aside. Combine butter, milk, and peanut butter chips in a small saucepan; cook over low heat, stirring constantly, until chips are melted and mixture is smooth. Remove from heat. Add warm mixture to sugar; stir in vanilla. Beat until smooth. Spread while frosting is warm.

Makes about 1 cup

black joe cake Black Joe Cake (also known as Black Midnight or Black Magic Cake) is a favorite of many families in Hershey and appears in just about every church, school, or community cookbook published in the area. Named for the brewed coffee that's a key ingredient, it is often complemented by a peanut butter icing. This version and the frosting recipe below come from professional caterer Colette McNitt, co-owner of Events Etc. by the Hershey Pantry in Hershey, Pennsylvania.

2 cups flour

2 cups sugar

3/4 cup cocoa

2 teaspoons baking soda

1/2 teaspoon salt

1 teaspoon baking powder

2 eggs

1/2 cup oil

1 cup milk

1 cup hot, brewed coffee, black

1. Mix dry ingredients in a large bowl until thoroughly combined. Slowly add the wet ingredients, adding the hot coffee last. Mix until all ingredients are well blended (batter will be thin).

2. Pour into two greased and floured 10-inch cake pans or one 13 x 9-inch pan. Bake at 350°F for 25 to 35 minutes, until cake tester comes out clean.

Serves 10 to 12

peanut butter frosting

2 cups vegetable shortening such as Crisco

3/4 cup margarine, softened to spreading consistency

1 cup peanut butter

1 tablespoon vanilla

1/2 cup milk

2 pounds confectioners' sugar

1. Cream together the shortening, margarine, and peanut butter. Add vanilla. Add milk alternately with confectioners' sugar. Beat at high speed for 2 minutes.

Frosts 2 (10-inch) cake layers or 1 (13 x 9-inch) sheet cake

texas sheet cake

Like the Black Joe Cake, this chocolate confection has a prized place in many local family recipe files. This version comes from the *Kooking for Kids* cookbook put together in 1980 by the houseparents of the Milton Hershey School. No one seems to know exactly why the cake is named for the Lone Star State, but its deep, dark flavor and moist texture make it a universal hit. Because it's so rich, a little goes a long way, so this is the perfect dessert for picnics, parties, or potlucks. Be sure to ice the cake while it's still hot to ensure a smooth finish.

2 sticks (¹/₂ pound) margarine

1 cup water

4 tablespoons cocoa

2 cups flour

2 cups sugar

¹/₂ teaspoon salt

2 eggs

¹/₂ cup sour cream

1 teaspoon baking soda

1 stick (¹/₄ pound) margarine

4 tablespoons cocoa

6 tablespoons milk

1 box confectioners' sugar

1 teaspoon vanilla

chopped nuts for decoration,
    if desired

1. Bring to a boil 2 sticks margarine, water, and 4 tablespoons cocoa; pour into a mixing bowl. Beat in flour, 2 cups sugar, and salt. Add eggs, sour cream, and baking soda; beat until smooth. Pour batter onto a greased 18 x 12-inch jelly-roll pan or cookie sheet with sides. Bake at 350°F for 20 to 25 minutes. Frost while still hot from the oven. Cool, then cut into squares.

2. To make the frosting: Bring to a boil 1 stick margarine, 4 tablespoons cocoa, and 6 tablespoons milk. Add the sugar and vanilla. (You'll know when you've added enough sugar when the mixture is of spreading consistency.) Frost hot cake and, if desired, top with nuts.

Serves 40 or more

Pack a Picnic

All work and no play was definitely not Milton Hershey's idea of a good life for the company employees who lived in the town he had built. So in 1907 he opened the park for their recreational enjoyment and added a picnic pavilion and zoo in 1910. Today town residents and visitors can still picnic in Hershey at first-come, first-served tables located beneath the Hersheypark Stadium (when there are no games or concerts scheduled) or at the tables provided on the patio area between the Hershey Museum and the park. You can even bring along your tabletop grill.

wacky cake

wacky cake You can't talk about favorite Hershey, Pennsylvania, desserts without including this easy-to-make treat that earned this crazy nickname (also known as Three Holes Cake) for two very good reasons. First, it has no eggs. Second, it needs no bowl to prepare. You just mix together the dry ingredients in the bottom of an ungreased square pan, then poke three holes in the mixture—one for the vanilla, one for the vinegar, and one for the salad oil. Mix in a cup of water and you're ready to bake.

With its popularity and ease of preparation and serving, it's no wonder the houseparents at the Milton Hershey School found this recipe worthy of inclusion in their 1980 *Kooking for Kids* cookbook. Don't worry about icing—just serve the warm squares with a little ice cream or give the cake a dusting of confectioners' sugar after it has cooled.

$1^1/_2$ cups sifted flour

1 cup sugar

3 tablespoons cocoa

1 teaspoon baking soda

$^1/_2$ teaspoon salt

1 teaspoon vanilla

1 teaspoon vinegar

5 tablespoons salad oil

1 cup cold water

1. Sift together dry (first five) ingredients into an ungreased 8-inch square pan. Make three depressions in the dry ingredient layer. Pour the vanilla into the first depression, the vinegar into the second depression, and the salad oil into the third. Pour the water into the pan and mix all of the ingredients together.

2. Bake in 350°F oven for 25 to 30 minutes.

Serves 8 to 10

Hershey's creamy cocoa pudding

The ultimate comfort food, chocolate pudding brings back fond memories with each soothing spoonful. This particular recipe, which originated in Hershey's Kitchens, dates from the late 1920s or early 1930s and continues to remind Susan Fowler, executive director of the Hershey Theatre, of times past and of longtime friends. Introduced at the Hershey Community Inn (later known as the Cocoa Inn), the pudding became a treasured tradition for the family of Alma Louise Payne Bobb, who came to Hershey when she married James Edward Bobb, who would become president and CEO of Hershey Estates (now known as Hershey Entertainment & Resorts). Alma Bobb had this same dessert served at her ninetieth birthday celebration in 2003. Susan Fowler recalls how pleased she was to receive the recipe from Mrs. Bobb ("who was regarded as a fine cook and hostess," says Fowler) to commemorate the occasion of her own marriage in 1978.

3 cups milk

$^{1}/_{2}$ cup minus 1 tablespoon HERSHEY'S
   unsweetened cocoa

$1^{1}/_{4}$ cups granulated sugar

$^{1}/_{4}$ teaspoon salt

$^{1}/_{4}$ cup cornstarch

3 tablespoons butter

$1^{1}/_{2}$ teaspoons vanilla

1. Scald milk in the top of a double boiler. Mix the dry ingredients together and add to the scalded milk; stir until blended. Cook over low heat, stirring occasionally, until mixture begins to thicken. Cover and continue to cook for 15 minutes.

2. Remove from heat; add butter and vanilla, stirring until butter is melted. Cover and chill, stirring occasionally.

   Serves 6 or more

Hershey's chocolate tapioca

Old-fashioned doesn't have to be out of date. This comforting creation from the 1932 *55 Recipes for Hershey's Syrup* promotional cookbook has stood the tests of time and taste.

3 cups milk

3 tablespoons sugar

6 tablespoons HERSHEY'S syrup

$^{1}/_{2}$ teaspoon salt

4 tablespoons quick-cooking tapioca

$^{1}/_{2}$ teaspoon vanilla

whipped cream

miniature chips or chocolate shavings

1. Bring milk to boiling point over boiling water in a double boiler; add sugar, syrup, and salt and stir in the tapioca; cook until the tapioca is clear. Cool; add vanilla and pour into serving dishes. Chill and top with whipped cream and miniature chips or chocolate shavings.

Makes 6 (4-ounce) servings

chocolate rice pudding

Another comfort classic from the *55 Recipes for Hershey's Syrup* booklet.

$^{1}/_{4}$ cup uncooked rice (not quick-cooking rice)

2 cups hot milk

$^{1}/_{2}$ teaspoon salt

$^{1}/_{3}$ cup sugar

$^{1}/_{2}$ cup raisins

1 tablespoon butter

3 tablespoons HERSHEY'S syrup

2 eggs, separated

$^{1}/_{2}$ teaspoon vanilla

4 tablespoons sugar

2 tablespoons HERSHEY'S unsweetened cocoa

1. Boil the rice in a quart of water until tender, then rinse and add to the hot milk with the salt, $^{1}/_{3}$ cup sugar, and raisins; bring to boiling point and add the butter, Hershey's syrup, egg yolks (reserve the whites for meringue), and vanilla.

2. Turn the mixture out into a buttered pudding dish and bake at 350°F for about 35 minutes. (If the mixture is too thick to pour into the dish, add a little more milk.)

3. Make a meringue of the egg whites, 4 tablespoons sugar, and cocoa. Spread meringue over cooked pudding. Place under broiler until lightly browned.

Makes 6 (4-ounce) servings

chocolate raspberry bread

Weekend mornings are the perfect time for families to linger over leisurely breakfasts and brunches, especially when you bring something homemade and chocolaty to the table. Will McQueen bakes batches of this lovely loaf to serve to guests at his 1825 Inn Bed and Breakfast in Palmyra, a tiny town right next door to Hershey.

1 package vanilla cake mix (use one
    to which you add your own butter)

4-ounce package instant chocolate
    pudding

3 tablespoons raspberry jam

8 ounces sour cream

4 eggs

1/4 cup oil

1/2 cup chocolate chips

1/2 cup chopped pecans

3 tablespoons flour

1. Preheat oven to 350°F and grease two loaf pans. Mix all of the ingredients together, then divide batter between the two prepared loaf pans. Bake for 40 to 50 minutes, until tops of loaves are golden. Cool in pans on wire racks for about 15 minutes. Remove loaves from pans and continue cooling on racks.

Makes 2 loaves

Happy Birthday, Mr. Hershey

More than 12,000 people turned out for Milton Hershey's eightieth birthday party, held at the Hershey Sports Arena in 1937. Frank P. Simione's reminiscences are among the oral histories recorded in the Hershey Community Archives. As he recalled:

"I attended both of his [Milton S. Hershey's] birthdays, when he was eighty and eight-five at the arena, and I remember it. . . . I remember the big cake. I remember the cocoa drinks. . . . I was only eleven years old. This was a thrill. They used to give candy Kisses out and . . . they had pans of chocolate cake that was made at the bakery. Hershey bakery in those days."

chocolate chip banana walnut bread

Another loaf to love, this one from Charlie Gipe, executive chef for the Hershey Entertainment Complex (including Hersheypark and the Giant Center).

1½ cups flour

½ teaspoon salt

1 cup sugar

1 teaspoon baking soda

¼ cup vegetable oil

2 eggs, well beaten

1¼ cups mashed bananas

⅜ cup HERSHEY'S semisweet chocolate chips

½ cup chopped walnuts

1. Preheat oven to 350°F. Grease and flour a loaf pan. Mix flour, salt, sugar, and baking soda in a large bowl. Mix in oil, eggs, and bananas. Stir in chocolate chips and walnuts. Pour into prepared loaf pan.

2. Bake for 70 minutes. Check for doneness with a toothpick; if the toothpick comes out clean, the loaf is done. Let cool for 15 minutes in pan, then turn out onto a wire rack to cool completely.

Makes 1 loaf

Friend Becomes Family

Although Milton Hershey was certainly the best-known candy maker in his namesake town, he wasn't the only one. Around 1917 Harry Burnett (known as "Poppy" to his family and "H.B." to everyone else) Reese came to Hershey to work on a dairy farm in response to a newspaper ad placed by Milton Hershey. Reese began making candy in his home basement after the farm closed. Prompted by promising sales, in 1926 he built a home and factory on West Caracas Avenue across from the Hershey plant, and in 1928 he introduced peanut butter cups covered with chocolate he purchased from Milton Hershey's company. A year after Reese's death in 1956, his six sons built a 10,000-square-foot production facility on Chocolate Avenue on the western edge of Hershey. Seven years later Hershey Chocolate Corporation acquired its friendly competitor.

chocolate and peanut butter praline pie

What's good in a candy cup is even better in a pie shell. This recipe from the Hershey-Derry Township Historical Society's *Hershey Centennial Cookbook,* submitted by local resident and member Joanne Lewis Curry, takes a winning combination of flavors to a whole new level of fun.

¾ cup packed light brown sugar

½ cup sugar

3 tablespoons flour

2 eggs

1 tablespoon milk

1 teaspoon vanilla

⅓ cup butter or margarine, melted

1 cup pecan pieces

½ cup HERSHEY'S semisweet
   chocolate chips

½ cup REESE'S peanut butter chips

1 unbaked 9-inch piecrust

vanilla ice cream or whipped topping
   (optional)

1. Preheat oven to 375°F. Stir together brown sugar, sugar, and flour in a medium bowl. Beat in eggs, milk, vanilla, and melted butter or margarine. Stir in pecan pieces, chocolate chips, and peanut butter chips.

2. Pour into piecrust. Bake for 35 to 40 minutes or just until set and golden brown. Cool completely on wire rack. Serve with ice cream or whipped topping if desired.

Makes 8 servings

Hershey-Derry Township Historical Society

In addition to the Hershey Community Archives, a major repository for historic information is the Hershey-Derry Township Historical Society, located at 40 Northeast Drive (behind the Hershey Outlets near Hersheypark, in the barn at the old Milton Hershey School home and farm). The society building houses collections of printed, oral, and genealogical histories and objects dating to the earliest settlements. It is also the site of a museum featuring Native American artifacts, early farm implements and household utensils, and an exhibit called Before There Was Chocolate, There Was Stone, which highlights the area's days as a major supplier of brownstone used for construction in cities from New York to St. Louis.

kid stuff

If a love of chocolate was one of the legacies handed down by Milton Hershey to his namesake town, a love of children was another. Although Milton and his wife, Catherine, were unable to have any of their own, the couple poured their own parental devotion—and a substantial amount of their personal wealth—into providing for the health, welfare, and education of disadvantaged young people.

Their primary focus at that time was orphaned boys, because boys were often left homeless, while girls were taken in by other family members. In 1909 the couple established the Milton Hershey Industrial School on 486 acres of Derry Township farmland to provide orphaned boys with a solid education and vocation.

The school meant so much to the Hersheys that in 1918, three years after Catherine died, Milton donated his entire personal fortune (including $60 million in Hershey Chocolate Company stock) to the school and set up the Hershey Trust Company, an independent firm, to manage the investments and to ensure that his business would continue to support the school in perpetuity. Today the Hershey Trust is valued at more than $7 billion (it owns 30 percent of the Hershey Company and 100 percent of Hershey Entertainment & Resorts).

Now known simply as the Milton Hershey School (MHS), this largest residential educational institution of its kind (pre-K through grade 12) in the United States, now on a 9,000-acre campus, provides its diverse student body with education, career training, housing, clothing, meals, health care, and counseling—all at no cost to their families. About half of the more than 1,300 students (enrollment is expected to grow to 1,800 in the foreseeable future) are girls. No longer restricted to orphans, students are selected on the basis of financial and social need.

Local residents would paddle canoes on Spring Creek in Hershey Park (now known as Hersheypark). This photo was taken around 1920.

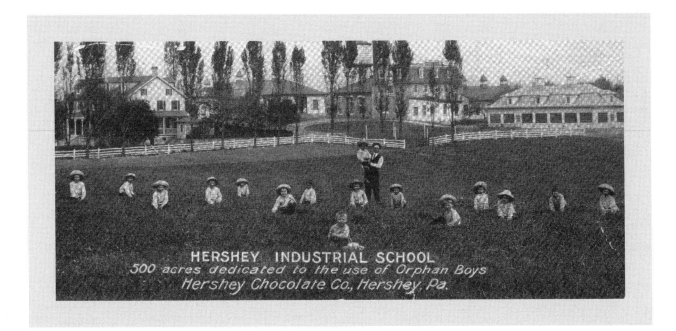

HERSHEY INDUSTRIAL SCHOOL
500 acres dedicated to the use of Orphan Boys
Hershey Chocolate Co., Hershey, Pa.

Although childless themselves, Milton and Catherine Hershey were committed to providing a solid educational foundation for the next generation.

The rest of the Hershey community was not forgotten in the distribution of its founder's fortune. The couple set up other trust funds. One is dedicated to supporting the public school system of Derry Township. The other, named the M.S. Hershey Foundation, funds the Hershey Theatre, Hershey Museum, Hershey Gardens, and Hershey Community Archives.

While education has always been a high priority in Hershey, family fun has also been a major part of the quality-of-life equation. And no place fills the fun bill better than Hersheypark.

Although Milton Hershey's practical mother thought the idea "frivolous," he was determined to create a "picnic and pleasure grounds" in town where his factory employees and their families could relax. The idea started modestly in 1907 with the opening of a landscaped park with plenty of lush spots for picnicking, calm waters for canoeing, and swings and slides for the little ones in

From the beginning Hershey Park (now known as Hersheypark) provided state-of-the-art excitement for local residents and out-of-town visitors, such as the Custer Car Ride from 1936 to 1940 (right).

The thrills at today's Hersheypark range from the high-flying Ferris wheel (left) to heart-stopping roller coasters.

Snow, Cocoa, and Cookies

Earl Houser moved to Hershey in 1920 when he was three years old. The Hershey Community Archives oral histories collection contains Houser's childhood memories of Milton Hershey: "In the winter when the snow was on the ground, we used to do our sleigh-riding and coasting on the hill to the north side of the [High Point] mansion. Occasionally, he [Milton Hershey] would send his chef out to invite us into the kitchen and have some cocoa and some cookies. At that time, we never saw the man. He would station himself in a window, and then he'd issue the orders to the chef, but we didn't see him."

1907. Fans could cheer on their favorite baseball teams from the grandstand of the new athletic field and be entertained by vaudeville and theater productions at the bandstand and pavilion.

Under a sign that urged YE WHO ENTER HERE LEAVE DULL CARES BEHIND, the park grew with the addition of a merry-go-round in 1908 and an amphitheater, two bowling alleys, a tennis court, a scenic railroad ride, and other attractions in subsequent years. Each year brought expansion and excitement to the community playground. Today, the 100-acre Hersheypark (the two words were joined in 1971) has become one of the nation's premier theme parks, attracting many of the five million people who visit the town of Hershey each year.

In 1946 Hershey Park introduced the Comet, which is still considered one of the nation's top wooden roller coasters. The Sooperdooperlooper, which took its first hair-raising ride in 1977, was the first steel looping roller coaster on the East Coast. Lightning Racer, the country's first racing/dueling coaster, made its debut in 2000. Then came the 65-foot pendulum ride called the Claw, the first of its kind in the Northeast, followed the next year by Storm Runner, the world's first hydraulic launch coaster. Today Hersheypark offers ten major coaster experiences. One of the flashiest rides opened in 2006: the Reese's Xtreme Cup Challenge, in which laser blaster–wielding teams in cars vie to hit targets as they speed through a series of sports-themed competitive zones.

Hersheypark opened its first water flume ride, the Mill Chute, in 1929. As America's love of water-oriented amusement rides grew over the years, so did the number of them at Hersheypark. By 2006 there were eight different splashy experiences ranging from the supertame Tiny Timbers to the moderate Roller Soaker to the high-intensity Canyon River Rapids, Coal Cracker, and Tidal Force.

Milton S. Hershey (at left) enjoyed the pleasures of the community he created. In this photo taken between 1935 and 1940, he takes a moment to share a snack with a friend at the Hershey Park Zoo.

To coincide with the park's centennial in 2007, Hershey Entertainment & Resorts introduced the Boardwalk at Hersheypark, a 4.6-acre addition that features five new water-based attractions. Among them are East Coast Waterworks, billed as the world's largest water-play structure. It uses 225 feet of bridges, seven slides, two crawl tunnels, and more than 300 interactive water toys for maximum wow power.

Of the sixty-plus rides and attractions in Hersheypark, some may be too intense for small children. To determine if a particular ride is appropriate for young ones, each is marked with a height range. For example, if you see Kisses chocolates or Hershey's Miniatures candies, the rides are okay for the kiddies.

Hershey chocolate chip cookie s'mores

When Hershey area native Charlie Gipe was about ten years old, he joined the local Boy Scout troop. Finding the campfire fare a bit lackluster, he was inspired to do a good deed for his troop mates and their leaders. He started cooking for them . . . all thirty of them. Gipe roasted wieners and made a mean chili. But what he really enjoyed doing were desserts such as Dutch oven cobblers and, of course, s'mores.

He still does. Only now Charlie Gipe is an American Culinary Federation Certified Chef who oversees all of the culinary activities at Hershey Entertainment Complex, which includes, among other properties, Hersheypark, Giant Center, and ZooAmerica. And his s'mores reflect his Hershey upbringing, because they're made with chocolate chip cookies instead of graham crackers!

On cookout nights at Hershey Lodge and Hershey Highmeadow Campground, guests can get "s'more kits," which are individual paper bags filled with marshmallows ready for roasting along with chocolate bars and either cookies or graham crackers for squooshing.

1 cup butter-flavored Crisco shortening

1¼ cups brown sugar

¾ cup sugar

1 teaspoon vanilla

2 whole eggs

2¼ cups unsifted flour

1 teaspoon baking soda

1 teaspoon salt

4 cups HERSHEY'S chocolate chips

large marshmallows (1 per s'more)

HERSHEY'S milk chocolate bars

1. Cream together in a large mixing bowl the shortening, brown sugar, sugar, and vanilla. In a separate bowl, beat eggs and add to mixture.

2. In a separate bowl, mix together flour, baking soda, and salt; add gradually to shortening mixture. Stir in chocolate chips. Drop batter by well-rounded teaspoons onto greased cookie sheets. Bake at 325°F for 8 minutes until barely brown.

3. To assemble the s'mores: For each s'more you'll need 1 large marshmallow, toasted on a campfire or grill, ¼ or ½ Hershey's milk chocolate bar (to taste), and 2 chocolate chip cookies. Squish together and eat!

Makes 7 to 8 dozen cookies

s'more pops

It's about a one-and-three-quarter-hour drive from Eileen Talanian's home in suburban Philadelphia to Hershey, but it's one she fondly recalls taking many times with her two children, Ben and Emily. To bring some of the fun home, Eileen is a professional baker, author of the cookbook *Chewy Cookies,* and creator of the Webzine howthecookiecrumbles.com. She came up with this easy-to-make Hershey chocolate-covered treat.

24 large marshmallows

4 HERSHEY'S milk chocolate bars

4 graham cracker rectangles

1. Push a wooden skewer into each marshmallow to make a "lollipop" and place it on a large dinner plate.

2. Place the chocolate bars into a saucepan and melt them over very low heat, stirring constantly, or place them in a bowl and microwave at 50% power for 1-minute intervals, stirring between each interval until the bars are melted.

3. Put the graham crackers into a plastic bag, flatten it to remove the air, and seal it. Use your hand, a rolling pin, or a box of cereal to crush the crackers to the size of rice grains. You don't want the crumbs to be too fine.

4. Set the marshmallows, then the melted chocolate, then the opened bag of graham crumbs, in that order, on the table.

5. Dip each skewered marshmallow into the chocolate to completely cover it; tap the skewer on the side of the bowl to let any excess chocolate drip off. Roll the skewered, chocolate-covered marshmallow into the graham cracker crumbs, turning it to coat it completely. Place it on another large dinner plate until the chocolate sets.

Makes 24 pops

Supersize My S'more, Please

Eight thousand Hershey's milk chocolate bars were used to make the world's biggest s'more in Los Angeles in 2003. Twenty thousand marshmallows and 25,000 graham crackers made up the rest of this stupendous-sized, squooshy sandwich.

no-bake chocolate oatmeal cookies

Quick and easy, these stovetop sweets were shared by Milton Hershey School houseparents in their 1980 *Kooking for Kids* cookbook.

2 cups sugar

$\frac{1}{4}$ cup HERSHEY'S unsweetened cocoa

$\frac{1}{2}$ cup butter

$\frac{1}{2}$ cup milk

$1\frac{1}{2}$ cups oatmeal (regular or quick cooking)

$1\frac{1}{2}$ cups coconut

1 teaspoon vanilla

1. Combine first four ingredients in a saucepan and boil for 5 minutes; remove from heat. Add oatmeal, coconut, and vanilla. Drop by tablespoonful onto waxed paper. Cool and serve.

Makes 3 to $3\frac{1}{2}$ dozen cookies

CHEF NOTE: If your youngsters aren't fond of coconut, you can substitute 3 cups oatmeal and $\frac{1}{2}$ cup peanut butter for the $1\frac{1}{2}$ cups oatmeal and $1\frac{1}{2}$ cups coconut.

Fun "Fore" Kids

The first golf course in the nation to welcome players under the age of eighteen was Spring Creek, a nine-hole course opened in 1934 by Milton S. Hershey. Originally called the Juvenile Golf Club, the par 33 course cost thirty-five cents to play. The name was changed to Spring Creek Golf Course—after its most prominent natural water hazard—in 1969.

Spring Creek Golf Course, operated by Hershey Entertainment & Resorts, underwent a recent renovation, including three new hole designs, restoration of the remaining six, and a 220-yard increase in course length (total now is 2,200). The addition of another set of tee boxes allows for variation of play for an eighteen-hole experience.

yum-yum squares

This chocolaty variation of the children's classic Rice Krispies Treat was attributed to Mrs. Gertrude Wisler in the 1955 cookbook *Recipes Worth Crowing About* published by the members of Fishburn's Evangelical United Brethren Church (now Fishburn United Methodist Church) on Fishburn Road in Hershey.

1 pound marshmallows

1 (6-ounce) package semisweet
  chocolate chips

3 tablespoons butter

$1/2$ teaspoon salt

1 teaspoon vanilla

$1^1/2$ cups Rice Krispies cereal

1 cup chopped nuts

1. Melt marshmallows, chocolate chips, and butter in the top of a double boiler. Add salt and vanilla; stir to blend. Combine cereal and nuts in a large bowl. Pour marshmallow and chocolate mixture over cereal and nuts; mix quickly.

2. Spread into a buttered 8-inch square pan. Chill in refrigerator for several hours or overnight. Cut into squares.

Makes about 9 squares

no-bake chocolate coconut balls

Another old favorite from an undated issue of Hershey's Kitchens' *Chocolate Town Bulletin.*

2 cups vanilla wafer crumbs (about 65
  vanilla wafers)

1 cup ($3^1/2$-ounce can) flaked coconut

1 cup confectioners' sugar

$3/4$ cup HERSHEY'S syrup

$1^1/2$ teaspoons vanilla

additional confectioners' sugar

1. To prepare vanilla wafer crumbs, grind up wafer cookies in a blender or place about 15 wafers at a time in double plastic bags and roll with a rolling pin.

2. Combine crumbs, coconut, and 1 cup confectioners' sugar in a large mixing bowl. Add chocolate syrup and vanilla to crumb mixture; mix thoroughly with hands until all dry ingredients are completely moistened.

3. Shape chocolate mixture into 1-inch balls and roll in confectioners' sugar. Store cookies in a waxed paper–lined airtight container. Reroll in confectioners' sugar before serving.

Makes about 3 dozen cookies

Hershey's chocolate french toast

You wouldn't be surprised to find chocolate chip pancakes on the breakfast buffet at Lebbie Lebkicher's, a casual dining spot in the Hershey Lodge named for one of Milton Hershey's closest lifelong friends and supporters. But what about Chocolate French Toast topped with Chocolate Whipped Butter? Hershey Lodge executive chef Bill Justus has to keep the batches coming when this dynamic duo shows up at the breakfast table.

When making this treat for kids, simply dot with whipped chocolate butter and a dusting of confectioners' sugar or a drizzle of warm maple syrup. For adults, bump up the sophistication factor with a Black Forest–style topping of canned pie cherries combined with about an ounce of your favorite fruit (kirschwasser cherry brandy is a natural) or nut liqueur.

4 eggs

2 tablespoons HERSHEY'S unsweetened cocoa

2 ounces HERSHEY'S SPECIAL DARK syrup

3 tablespoons sugar

1/4 cup milk

1/4 teaspoon vanilla

8 slices bread

2 tablespoons butter

1. Mix together eggs, cocoa, syrup, sugar, milk, and vanilla. Soak each bread slice in the mixture until fully coated.

2. Melt butter in a nonstick sauté pan and fry bread slices until golden brown. Add toppings and serve immediately.

Serves 4

Hershey's chocolate whipped butter

1 pound butter, softened

1 ounce HERSHEY'S syrup

1 tablespoon HERSHEY'S unsweetened cocoa

1. To softened butter, add syrup and cocoa powder. Whip until smooth.

Makes about 32 servings

Hershey's chocolate world dipped apples
At Hershey's Chocolate World visitor center, singing confectionery artists called "the Hersheyizers" jazz up cupcakes and brownies with different colored frostings and toppings of chips, pieces, sprinkles, and crumbles of candies that kids pick out themselves. The Hersheyizers also give apples the Hershey's chocolate treatment with a plunge into the attraction's special recipe coatings, a roll in candy, and some delectable drizzles of peanut butter or white chocolate.

Angela Gilbert, manager of the Hershey Bake Shoppe in Hershey's Chocolate World visitor center, shared this recipe, which can also be used to dip frozen bananas and pretzel rods. Dipping makes a fun at-home kid's party activity, too. You do the dunking and set out bowls of candy options to let youngsters decorate to their heart's content.

Granny Smith apples work particularly well because of the contrast of slightly sour fruit with sweet chocolate. Make sure the apples are cold so the chocolate coating will set up faster.

10 ounces butter

5 cups HERSHEY'S semisweet chocolate chips

1 tablespoon vanilla

1 cup corn syrup

5 cups REESE'S peanut butter chips

1 tablespoon vegetable oil

5 apples, chilled

5 sturdy lollipop sticks

1. To make the chocolate dip, combine butter, chocolate chips, vanilla, and corn syrup in the top of a double boiler. Heat, continually stirring, until chocolate chips and butter melt and the mixture is thoroughly blended.

2. To make the peanut butter dip: Melt the peanut butter chips in the top of a double boiler; stir in vegetable oil.

3. Place a lollipop stick in the stem end of each apple. You can dunk whole apples in one of these two mixtures or drizzle the peanut butter dip with a spoon to create fancy designs on apples you have already dipped in the semisweet chocolate.

Serves 5

chocolate fun dough At the Hershey Lodge a daily schedule of family-friendly activities is available to guests each morning. One of the most popular involves imaginative art play with modeling dough made from chocolate. Also known as modeling chocolate, this mixture is simple to make and is a moldable medium that little artists will love getting their hands into. While the dough is a bit too sweet for snacking on, it's certainly no problem if little Michelangelos can't resist a little munching.

10 ounces HERSHEY'S SPECIAL DARK
   chocolate chips

$1/3$ cup light corn syrup

1. Melt the chocolate chips in a microwave for 1 minute (stirring occasionally) or in the top of a double boiler until the chocolate becomes smooth and creamy. (You can also place the chocolate chips in a bowl over another bowl that contains hot, but not boiling, water.) Once the chocolate has melted, add the corn syrup and blend.

2. Pour the mixture onto a waxed paper sheet and spread it with your fingers until it's about $1/2$ inch thick. Cover loosely with waxed paper and let it stiffen for at least a couple of hours or overnight. The chocolate mixture will become very pliable.

Makes a 7-inch square of dough

Cool Critters

Make the dough-playing experience educational by asking children to mold their favorite animals and tell about where and how they live. They can get plenty of inspiration at ZooAmerica, where more than 200 animals native to the North American continent live in natural habitat settings. The eleven-acre zoo is one of the Hershey Entertainment & Resorts properties and is located right across an easily walkable bridge from Hersheypark. And how cool would your kid feel about creating a couple of chocolate coatis (cousin of the raccoon) or a long-tailed crocodile?

(H) chocolate caramel sauce Upon her engagement in 1932, the Hershey Chocolate Corporation sent a copy of its recipe booklet entitled *55 Recipes for Hershey's Syrup* to a young woman named Dorothy Shissler of Harrisburg, the capital of Pennsylvania, located about fifteen minutes away from the town of Hershey. The introduction of the book, which now resides in the Hershey Community Archives, was written to put new cooks' minds at ease by assuring them that "if some of the recipes in this booklet seem lengthy it is because they call for several ingredients. You will not need to 'fuss' with any of them, and you'll never have to 'fuss' with Hershey's Syrup. You will not need to melt it, shave it, or wait for it. Simply stir and use." Here's an ice-cream sundae topping from the booklet that can be served warm or cold.

1 cup brown sugar

dash salt

3 tablespoons water

4 tablespoons HERSHEY'S syrup

1 tablespoon butter

1 teaspoon cornstarch

1 cup boiling water

1/2 teaspoon vanilla

1. Cook brown sugar and salt with 3 tablespoons of water over low heat to a light caramel brown. Add chocolate syrup, then the butter and cornstarch mixed to a paste; then add the boiling water and the vanilla. Cook over boiling water in a double boiler until thick.

2. Serve over ice cream or other desserts.

Makes about 2½ cups

(H) chocolate whipped cream If you want to top your sundae off in true Hershey style, use this other selection from the Hershey's syrup recipe book. As the recipe says, "No sugar is required, as Hershey's Syrup will sweeten the cream sufficiently."

1 cup heavy cream

2 tablespoons HERSHEY'S syrup

1. Chill the cream thoroughly and whip until stiff enough to stand alone. Gradually fold in chocolate syrup.

Makes 1 cup

hot fudge sundae cake

(V) **hot fudge sundae cake** Here's a twist on the traditional chocolate sundae from the 1992 *Ladies of the Church* cookbook. This recipe was originally submitted by Tracy Hoy, a member of the Trinity Evangelical Lutheran Church in Colebrook, a close neighbor to Hershey.

1 cup flour

¾ cup sugar

2 tablespoons cocoa

2 teaspoons baking powder

¼ teaspoon salt

½ cup milk

2 tablespoons oil

1 teaspoon vanilla

1 cup chopped nuts

1 cup brown sugar

¼ cup cocoa

1¾ cups hot water

1. Preheat oven to 350°F. Mix flour, sugar, 2 tablespoons cocoa, baking powder, and salt in an ungreased 9-inch square pan. Mix in milk, oil, and vanilla with fork until smooth. Stir in nuts. Spread around in pan. Sprinkle with brown sugar and ¼ cup cocoa. Pour hot water over batter.

2. Bake for 40 minutes. While warm, spoon into dishes and top with ice cream. Spoon sauce from pan onto each serving.

Serves 8

Special Treatment

Jaymee Mehrmann was born in Hershey in 1956. These memories of her school days are recorded as oral history in the Hershey Community Archives: "It was so much fun in elementary school. We got to take a tour of the factory every year, and the neat thing was . . . the ladies at the Kiss line . . . they would let us fill our pockets full of candy right from the line. . . . And then we still got . . . a little candy bar or something from the tour guide."

chocolate and fruit snack mix

When the Hershey Chocolate Factory was open for public tours, local residents Joanne Lewis Curry and her sister worked as guides. One famous visitor who stands out in Joanne's mind was movie star Ginger Rogers. Although executives from the corporate office led Rogers's tour, Joanne and her colleagues did enjoy their own glimmer of Hollywood-style glamour by trying on the actress's luxurious coat. Today Joanne works with the Hershey-Derry Township Historical Society and, in 2003, chaired the publication of the organization's *Hershey Centennial Cookbook,* to which she submitted this snack mix.

½ cup (1 stick) butter or margarine

2 tablespoons sugar

1 tablespoon HERSHEY'S unsweetened cocoa

½ teaspoon ground cinnamon

3 cups bite-size crisp rice squares cereal

3 cups bite-size crisp wheat squares cereal

3 cups toasted oat cereal rings

1 cup cashews

1½ cups (6-ounce package) dried fruit bits

1 cup HERSHEY'S semisweet chocolate chips

1. Place butter or margarine in a 4-quart microwave-safe bowl. Microwave on high (100% power) for 1 minute or until melted; stir in sugar, cocoa, and cinnamon. Add cereals and cashews; stir until evenly coated. Microwave on high for 3 minutes, stirring at 1-minute intervals. Stir in dried fruit. Cool completely; stir in chocolate chips. Store in a tightly covered container in cool, dry place.

Makes about 11 cups of mix

Super Sipper

Here's a little tip from Lebbie Lebkicher's Restaurant at the Hershey Lodge for making chocolate milk extraspecial. Substitute a chocolate Twizzler's candy (with the ends snipped off) for the straw.

Mounds chocolate cupcakes
No icing is needed for this Hershey's Kitchens classic inspired by the coconut Mounds bar.

1 package (8 ounces) softened cream cheese

$\frac{1}{3}$ cup sugar

1 egg

$\frac{1}{2}$ teaspoon almond extract

$\frac{1}{8}$ teaspoon salt

1 cup MOUNDS sweetened coconut flakes

3 cups flour

2 cups sugar

$\frac{2}{3}$ cup HERSHEY'S unsweetened cocoa

2 teaspoons baking soda

1 teaspoon salt

2 cups water

$\frac{2}{3}$ cup vegetable oil

2 tablespoons white vinegar

2 teaspoons vanilla

1. To make the filling: Beat cream cheese, $\frac{1}{3}$ cup sugar, egg, almond extract, and $\frac{1}{8}$ teaspoon salt in a small bowl until smooth and creamy. Stir in coconut.

2. To make the cake: Stir together flour, 2 cups sugar, cocoa, baking soda, and 1 teaspoon salt in a large bowl. Add water, oil, vinegar, and vanilla; beat on medium speed of a mixer for 2 minutes.

3. Fill lined muffin cups $\frac{2}{3}$ full with batter. Spoon 1 level tablespoon of coconut filling into the center of each cupcake. Bake for 20 to 25 minutes or until a wooden pick inserted in the cake portion comes out clean. Remove from pan to wire rack and cool completely.

Makes $2\frac{1}{2}$ dozen cupcakes

chocolate-bar-filled chocolate cupcakes
Hershey milk chocolate bars lend their signature flavor to the fluffy filling of these totable treats created by Hershey's Kitchens.

1 (8-ounce) package cream cheese, softened

1/3 cup sugar

1 egg

1/8 teaspoon salt

1 (6-ounce) HERSHEY'S milk chocolate bar, cut into 1/4-inch pieces

3 cups all-purpose flour

2 cups sugar

2/3 cup HERSHEY'S unsweetened cocoa

2 teaspoons baking soda

1 teaspoon salt

2 cups water

2/3 cup vegetable oil

2 tablespoons white vinegar

2 teaspoons vanilla

2 (6-ounce) HERSHEY'S milk chocolate bars, broken into pieces

1. Preheat oven to 350°F. Line 2 1/2-inch muffin cups with paper baking cups.

2. To prepare filling: Beat cream cheese, 1/3 cup sugar, egg, and 1/8 teaspoon salt in a small bowl until smooth and creamy. Stir in 1 chocolate bar, cut into 1/4-inch pieces.

3. To prepare cake: Stir together flour, 2 cups sugar, cocoa, baking soda, and 1 teaspoon salt in a large bowl. Add water, oil, vinegar, and vanilla; beat on medium speed of a mixer for 2 minutes.

4. Fill muffin cups 2/3 full with batter. Spoon 1 level tablespoon of filling into the center of each cupcake. Bake for 20 to 25 minutes or until a wooden pick inserted in the cake portion comes out clean. Remove from pan to wire rack. Cool completely. Top each cupcake with a chocolate bar piece.

Makes about 2 1/2 dozen cupcakes

Cup a Cake

Just about any cake can be baked as cupcakes by following these guidelines offered by Hershey's Kitchens. Prepare the recipe as directed, but instead of baking in cake pans, fill paper-lined baking cups 1/2 to 3/4 full with batter and bake at 375°F for about 16 to 20 minutes. Expect a yield of about 1 1/2 to 2 dozen cupcakes from a recipe calling for about 2 1/4 cups of flour.

chocolate for dinner?

When visitors come to Hershey, Pennsylvania, they expect to find chocolate on the menu. But there's no need to wait for dessert to indulge. Chefs at the restaurants at the Hotel Hershey and Hershey Lodge use chocolate in just about all of its forms and flavors to add intrigue, complexity, and richness to all manner of dishes from appetizers to entrees, sauces, sides, and salads.

If you think Buffalo, New York, has the corner on cravable chicken wings, you haven't tasted the ones smothered in the smoky, deeply flavored barbecue sauce (guess the secret ingredient) served at the Hershey Grill. Like ketchup on your fries? At Lebbie Lebkicher's at the Hershey Lodge, the potato's best pal takes on a tangy new twist. Even the Italian classic risotto gets the Hershey treatment with the addition of Premier White Chips, and strip steak gets a regal crown of semisweet chips, diced tomatoes, and crumbles of pepper Jack cheese.

The use of chocolate in savory recipes is nothing new. In Mexico a slow-cooked, deep-flavored sauce called mole poblano, which has unsweetened chocolate as one of its key ingredients, has been traditional fiesta fare for hundreds of years. Some food historians say that the history of mole goes back as far as the late seventeenth century, when a group of nuns in the state of Puebla, about 60 miles southeast of Mexico City, used all of the finest chilies, spices, and other flavorings available in their pantry to whip up a tasty sauce to spruce up some turkey they had cooked for a visiting church official. *Mole poblano de guajolote* (turkey with mole poblano) is still extremely popular in Mexico (it is often referred to as the country's national dish) and is considered a food of celebration.

The Hotel Hershey maintains its original European ambience and style of service.

spiced chicken mole with salsa

Here's the Hershey's Kitchens take on the classic Mexican mole.

2 tablespoons ground coffee beans

2 tablespoons HERSHEY'S unsweetened cocoa

1 tablespoon brown sugar

1$\frac{1}{2}$ teaspoons salt

1 teaspoon chili powder

4 boneless, skinless chicken breasts

1 tablespoon vegetable oil

2 tomatoes, chopped

1 avocado, peeled and diced

1 green onion, minced

1 tablespoon snipped cilantro

1 clove garlic, pressed

$\frac{1}{4}$ cup HERSHEY'S Minichips semi-sweet chocolate chips

1 teaspoon lime juice

$\frac{1}{2}$ teaspoon salt (optional)

cilantro sprigs (optional)

rice (optional)

tortilla chips (optional)

1. Preheat oven to 425°F. Grease a baking sheet. Stir together ground coffee beans, cocoa, brown sugar, 1$\frac{1}{2}$ teaspoons salt, and chili powder. Rub chicken pieces with vegetable oil; pat on cocoa mixture. Place coated chicken pieces on a prepared baking sheet. Bake for 20 to 25 minutes or until juices are clear.

2. Meanwhile, prepare Special Salsa Mole: Stir together tomatoes, avocado, onion, cilantro, garlic, miniature chocolate chips, lime juice, and $\frac{1}{2}$ teaspoon salt, if desired, in a medium bowl.

3. Arrange chicken and salsa on plate. Garnish with cilantro sprigs, if desired. Serve with rice and tortilla chips, if desired.

Serves 4

chili con cocoa

Cocoa and Kisses milk chocolate make this the perfect party food. Serve this Hershey's Kitchens recipe in hollowed-out bread boules and let your guests try to guess your secret ingredients.

1/4 cup vegetable oil

1 1/2 cups chopped onion

2 pounds ground beef or ground turkey

2 tablespoons HERSHEY'S unsweetened cocoa

2 tablespoons chili powder

2 teaspoons ground cayenne pepper

1 teaspoon salt

1/2 teaspoon ground allspice

1/2 teaspoon ground cinnamon

7 cups whole tomatoes, undrained

1 1/3 cups tomato paste

1 cup water

1/2 cup HERSHEY'S MINI KISSES milk chocolates

3 cups dark red kidney beans, undrained

14 (8-ounce) mini bread boules, hollowed out

1. Heat oil over medium heat in a large saucepan; add onion. Cook, stirring frequently, for 3 minutes or until tender. Add meat; cook until brown. Drain. Stir in cocoa, chili powder, cayenne pepper, salt, allspice, cinnamon, tomatoes with liquid, tomato paste, and water; heat to boiling. Reduce heat. Add chocolate pieces and beans; simmer for 30 minutes. Ladle chili (about 1 cup each) into prepared bread boules. Garnish as desired.

Serves 14

Chocolate, of Course

Each winter Hershey Entertainment & Resorts kicks off its Chocolate-Covered February celebration with a Chocolate Dinner Extraordinaire in the Hotel Hershey Circular Dining Room. Each course from appetizer to dessert (salad dressing included) is made with a Hershey's chocolate product. A la carte chocolate dinners are also available at the hotel throughout the month.

Hershey's chocolate balsamic vinaigrette

Unless you know, you probably won't be able to put your finger on what makes this salad dressing served at the Hershey Grill so special.

1 tablespoon shallots, minced

1 teaspoon Dijon mustard

1½ cups olive oil

¾ cup balsamic vinegar

½ cup HERSHEY'S SPECIAL DARK syrup

salt and pepper to taste

1. In a stainless steel bowl, mix together shallots and mustard. Alternately add oil and vinegar, whisking constantly. Add all other ingredients; mix well.

Makes 1 quart

Hershey's chocolate, tomato, and pepper jack–crusted strip steak

The richness of a good strip steak, surprising bursts of chocolate, the bright acidity of tomatoes, and the creamy texture and peppery kick of the cheese make this a popular entree at the Hershey Grill. Take your taste buds beyond their preconceived notions. Try it and you'll crave it. Executive chef Bill Justus says that the crust is just as good on chicken or fish.

4 (12-ounce) strip steaks

1 cup pepper Jack cheese, crumbled

½ cup tomatoes, diced and seeded

⅓ cup diced onion

¼ cup chopped basil

½ teaspoon minced garlic

¼ cup HERSHEY'S semisweet chocolate chips

salt and pepper to taste

1. Broil the strip steak to your liking.

2. To make the crust: In a bowl, gently mix together the remaining ingredients. Divide crust ingredients into four equal portions and spread on top of steaks. Broil for about 1 minute or until cheese and chocolate chips melt (chips may retain their original form when melted).

Serves 4

Hershey's white chocolate risotto

White chips add more creaminess than sweetness to this extra-luxurious Hershey Lodge version of the Italian classic arborio rice dish.

4 tablespoons butter

1 medium yellow onion, diced

2 cups arborio rice

5 to 6 cups hot chicken broth or stock

salt and pepper to taste

$1/4$ cup HERSHEY'S Premier White Chips

1. Melt butter in a saucepan over medium heat. Add diced onion to butter and cook until soft and translucent. Once the onion is soft, add rice and cook over medium heat, stirring constantly. Do not brown the rice.

2. Add about $1/2$ cup hot chicken broth or stock to the pan with the rice, stirring with a wooden spoon. As the rice begins to cook, stir it constantly, making sure to scrape all the way to the bottom of the pan to prevent sticking. When you see little bubbles popping up from the liquid, turn the heat down to medium low. Continue adding broth or stock $1/2$ to $3/4$ cup at a time until the liquid is gone; this should take about 20 minutes.

3. Fold in the white chocolate chips.

Makes about 6 servings

Hershey's chocolate ketchup

You wouldn't expect visitors to Hershey to dunk their waffle fries in just any garden-variety ketchup. At Lebbie Lebkicher's restaurant inside the Hershey Lodge, the deeply colored dip is enriched with dark chocolate syrup.

4 cups ketchup

1 cup HERSHEY'S SPECIAL DARK chocolate syrup

1. Mix all ingredients together and place in an airtight container.

   Makes 5 cups

Hershey's chocolate barbecue sauce

Here's another favorite from Hershey Lodge. Brush it on wings, grilled chicken, pork, or steak. Think it's good the first day? Make extra to ensure at least some leftovers. If you can wait, the flavor's even better the next day.

1 small onion, diced

2 cloves garlic, minced

$\frac{1}{4}$ cup olive oil

1 tablespoon lemon juice

$\frac{1}{4}$ teaspoon salt

$\frac{1}{2}$ tablespoon black pepper

1 teaspoon paprika

$\frac{1}{2}$ teaspoon hot sauce

$1\frac{1}{2}$ cups ketchup

2 tablespoons prepared mustard

$\frac{1}{4}$ cup apple cider vinegar

$\frac{1}{4}$ cup HERSHEY'S syrup (regular or SPECIAL DARK)

1. In a saucepan, sauté onion and garlic in oil; cook until tender. Stir in lemon juice, salt, pepper, paprika, and hot sauce; simmer for 5 to 6 minutes. Reduce heat and stir in ketchup, mustard, vinegar, and chocolate syrup; simmer for 15 to 20 minutes more.

   Makes 1 quart of sauce

cocoa-seared scallops with vanilla-scented beurre blanc over braised fennel

This elegant appetizer is served at the Forebay Restaurant at the Hershey Lodge in a martini glass. It pairs exceptionally well with a Riesling wine.

2 tablespoons HERSHEY'S unsweetened cocoa

1 teaspoon allspice

$1/8$ teaspoon chili powder

$1/2$ teaspoon salt

$1/2$ teaspoon ground pepper

12 scallops

2 cups heavy cream

1 cup white wine

$1/2$ cup fresh squeezed lemon juice

10 whole black peppercorns

1 vanilla bean (cut in half)

2 tablespoons minced shallots

1 pound butter, cut into pieces

1 head fennel, finely julienned (use the bulb and reserve the tops for soup or garnish)

$1/4$ cup olive oil

$1/2$ cup white wine

1 cup vegetable or chicken stock

salt and pepper to taste

1. Begin by making the Cocoa Spice Rub: Combine cocoa powder, allspice, chili powder, salt, and pepper. Dredge scallops in cocoa rub. Sear scallops on medium-high heat for 2 minutes per side.

2. To prepare Vanilla-Scented Beurre Blanc: Heat cream in a heavy saucepan over medium-high heat; cook until it is reduced to $3/4$ cup. In another saucepan, add 1 cup white wine, lemon juice, peppercorns, vanilla bean halves, and shallots; reduce until almost dry. Add heavy cream and slowly incorporate the butter, one piece at a time. Strain the mixture.

3. Brown fennel in olive oil over medium heat; deglaze pan with wine by scraping the browned bits off the bottom with a wooden spoon before adding $1/2$ cup white wine. Reduce heat to medium, then add stock and seasoning. Cover and braise until tender.

4. To assemble: Place $1/4$ of the braised fennel in a martini glass; top with three scallops and $1/4$ of the beurre blanc. Garnish with microgreens.

Serves 4

cocoa-crusted snapper with mango salsa

The Hershey Lodge Cocoa Spice Rub that turns scallops into stars can have the same stellar effect on snapper.

4 (6-ounce) skinless snapper filets

1 recipe Cocoa Spice Rub (see page 67)

$\frac{1}{2}$ cup oil

2 mangos, peeled and diced small

1 small red onion, diced

$\frac{1}{2}$ cup cilantro, chopped

$\frac{1}{2}$ tablespoon hot sauce

$\frac{1}{2}$ tablespoon jalapeño pepper, chopped

juice of two limes

$\frac{1}{4}$ cup HERSHEY'S SPECIAL DARK chocolate chips

2 tablespoons olive oil

salt and pepper to taste

1. Dredge each snapper filet in Cocoa Spice Rub. Sear on medium-high heat in oil for 4 minutes per side.

2. Meanwhile, prepare the Mango Salsa by combining all remaining ingredients in a medium bowl. Stir well. Arrange salsa on plate next to snapper filet.

Serves 4

No Corners, Please

There's good reason why Milton Hershey wanted the white-tablecloth dining room in the hotel that bears his name to be round. "In some places, if you don't tip well, they put you in a corner," Hershey said. "I don't want any corners." Ditto for pillars, which could obstruct guests' views of the surrounding gardens and scenic Pennsylvania hills.

This early 1920s promotional poster portrayed chocolate as a classy snack.

HERSHEY'S
Milk Chocolate

A Meal In Itself

MADE IN HERSHEY, PA., "THE CHOCOLATE AND COCOA TOWN"

cocoa-seared scallops with burnt orange sauce Scallops also
take the spotlight in this signature appetizer from the Hotel Hershey.

1¹/₂ cups HERSHEY'S unsweetened
   cocoa

2 teaspoons ground nutmeg

¹/₂ cup ground white pepper

2 tablespoons ancho chili pepper
   powder

4 teaspoons sesame seeds

1 teaspoon ground cinnamon

1 tablespoon paprika

8 ounces shallots, chopped

4 ounces garlic, chopped

1 tablespoon whole black peppercorns

kosher salt, to taste

pepper, to taste

¹/₄ cup parsley, chopped

¹/₄ cup fresh thyme, chopped

1 cup white wine

2 quarts orange juice from concentrate

1 quart heavy cream

1 tablespoon kosher salt

2 teaspoons confectioners' sugar

3 large scallops per serving (12 total)

1. To prepare the Cocoa Crust: Combine cocoa, nutmeg, white pepper, chili powder, sesame, cinnamon, and paprika. Set aside.

2. To prepare the Burnt Orange Sauce: Sweat shallots and garlic in a heavy-bottom saucepan (cook over low heat until soft and transparent). Add peppercorns, salt and pepper to taste, parsley, and thyme; sweat an additional 5 minutes. Deglaze the pan with wine (scrape up the taste-intensive browned bits from the bottom of the pan, add wine, and swish around the pan). Add orange juice; reduce until mixture produces a thickened caramel texture. Add heavy cream. Simmer for 45 minutes; strain and cool.

3. To prepare scallops: Combine 1 tablespoon salt and 2 teaspoons confectioners' sugar. Dust scallops in salt mixture, then dust in Cocoa Crust mixture. Sear scallops in a skillet until they become white and firm (don't overcook). Drizzle Burnt Orange Sauce over cooked scallops. Garnish with microgreens tossed in olive oil, salt, and pepper

Serves 4

AUTHOR NOTE: You can use about 1¹/₂ teaspoons of olive oil to sauté the scallops. Do not use extra virgin olive oil, because it burns at high temperatures.

chocolate dutch oven stew

Whoever said opposites attract must have had Hershey native (and corporate chef) Charlie Gipe and his wife, Patti, in mind. He likes milk chocolate and she prefers dark, but they obviously share other common ground because they've been married for twenty-five years and counting. An outdoor enthusiast, Charlie likes to make this hearty stew over a campfire.

3 tablespoons butter

2 pounds stew meat, cut into 1-inch cubes

3 tablespoons flour

salt and pepper to taste

1 medium onion, diced

$\frac{1}{2}$ cup carrots, peeled and diced

1 cup celery, diced

1 cup potatoes, diced

2 quarts chicken stock

2 (8-ounce) cans whole tomatoes in sauce

2 (8-ounce) cans diced tomatoes in sauce

2 tablespoons HERSHEY'S unsweetened cocoa

1. Melt butter in a Dutch oven. Meanwhile, toss stew meat cubes, flour, and salt and pepper in a large bowl. Place the mixture in the Dutch oven and brown meat for about 15 minutes. Add onion, carrots, celery, and potatoes to the Dutch oven; cook over medium-high heat until onions are tender.

2. Add chicken stock and whole and diced tomatoes to the Dutch oven; bring to a boil and reduce heat to simmer for 1 hour. Add cocoa and cook for another 30 minutes or until beef is tender.

Makes ¾ gallon

Scharffen Berger cacao nib rub on tri-tip roast

In 2005 the Hershey Company acquired Scharffen Berger, a Berkeley, California—based maker of premium dark chocolates, to expand its presence in the high-end gourmet chocolate market. Among Scharffen Berger's signature products are its cacao nibs, the roasted hearts of the cacao beans. Crunchy and slightly nutty tasting, nibs add a light chocolate essence, without sweetness, to baked goods and savory dishes.

Chocolate adds an indefinable *mmm*-factor to grilled meats, such as tri-tip roast or skirt or flank steak. You can apply the rub any time from a few hours to the day before cooking. The longer, the better to allow the combination of spices to work their flavorful magic.

2 tablespoons SCHARFFEN BERGER cacao nibs

2 teaspoons dried red pepper flakes

1 teaspoon ground cumin

$1/2$ teaspoon ground (dry) mustard

$1/2$ teaspoon chili powder

$1/2$ teaspoon allspice

2 tablespoons brown sugar, packed

2 tablespoons kosher salt

1 $2^{1}/_{2}$ pound tri-tip roast (fat cap left on)

1. To make the rub: Combine all dry ingredients in the bowl of a food processor, spice grinder, or mortar and pestle. Grind until the nibs break into particles about the size of coarse cornmeal. Use immediately or store in a tightly covered jar for up to 1 month.

2. To prepare the roast: Rinse and pat the roast dry with paper towels. Generously cover the meat with the rub and wrap in foil or plastic wrap. The roast can marinate overnight in the refrigerator. Remove the roast from the refrigerator and bring to room temperature.

3. Fire up the grill. Prepare the grill for indirect cooking, with the coals to either side. Place the meat on the grill, fat side up, not directly over the coals. The internal grill temperature should be between 275°F and 300°F. Grill the meat for 40 minutes. Check the temperature with an instant-read thermometer. For medium-rare meat, remove from grill when the thermometer reads 125°F. Let the roast sit, loosely covered with foil, for several minutes before slicing.

Serves 6

Scharffen Berger spiced cocoa dry rub on lamb kabobs

Your nose can usually be trusted to pick up aroma cues. But in this instance smell can be deceiving. Although this rub is fragrant with chocolate, the flavor only hints of the presence of this versatile ingredient. You can apply the rub to lamb shoulder and leg cubes for grilled kabobs or use it to spice up a butterflied leg of lamb. This recipe, from Scharffen Berger Chocolate Maker, makes enough rub for five pounds of lamb.

1 cup **SCHARFFEN BERGER natural cocoa powder (unsweetened)**

¼ cup **kosher salt**

2 teaspoons **dried red pepper flakes, chopped fine**

½ teaspoon **ground cloves**

2 tablespoons **sugar**

4 pounds **lamb shoulder and/or leg, cut into 1½-inch cubes**

2 **red onions**

1. To make the rub: Combine dry ingredients in the bowl of a food processor, spice grinder, or mortar and pestle. Grind until the pepper flakes are crushed into a fine powder. Store leftovers in a tightly covered jar for up to 1 month.

2. To prepare the kabobs: Generously coat lamb cubes with the dry rub. Using metal skewers, alternate lamb cubes with pieces of red onion. Let the kabobs marinate for up to 12 hours or overnight in the refrigerator.

3. Light the grill. Remove the lamb from the refrigerator and bring to room temperature before grilling. Grill over direct coals, turning once after 5 minutes. If grill has a lid, cover the meat while it is grilling. Using an instant-read thermometer, check the internal temperature of the lamb cubes; for medium-rare meat, remove from the grill when the temperature reaches 125°F.

Makes 1½ cups

showstopping sweets

Much of the appeal of the Hershey, Pennsylvania, area is in its natural beauty—the gently rolling farmland and hilltop views that seem to go on forever. But some of the area's most spectacular sites sprang from designs of architects, the hands of local stone crafters and, most of all, the mind of Milton Hershey. Combining a lifelong respect for the quiet dignity of the landscape with a sophisticated aesthetic cultivated through world travel, Hershey brought a unique perspective to his plans for the town, particularly during his Great Building Campaign of the Great Depression.

When, for example, Hershey planned to construct a "Grand Hotel" for his town, he wanted to duplicate the exotic splendor of the Hotel Heliopolis in Cairo, Egypt, where he and his wife, Catherine, had spent some of their happiest times. He went as far as to arrange the purchase of the original hotel building plans from its architect. But those plans came to an abrupt end when Hershey's Pennsylvania architect estimated that it would cost in excess of $5 million to carry out the project.

Hershey didn't abandon his Grand Hotel vision; he simply amended it. Instead of the elaborately rendered blueprints of the Heliopolis, Hershey gave his architect a picture postcard showing the front view of a somewhat more modest, but still elegant, thirty-room, U-shaped hotel that he and Catherine had discovered while vacationing in the Mediterranean. Rather than thirty rooms, however, he wanted 170.

Although Hershey's mother dismissed even these plans as "hopelessly extravagant," he broke ground for his Mediterranean masterpiece in 1932. The Hotel Hershey opened the following May. Company historic

In summer the formal gardens surrounding the Hotel Hershey provide a lovely view from any vantage point, inside or out.

Resident Songsters

The balcony of the Fountain Lobby was once home to cages filled with colorful canaries whose songs would fill the room with cheerful sounds. The hotel hired a parlor maid whose sole job was to care for and feed the birds.

records quote a local newspaper's description of the new hotel as "characterized by a great luxury of detail and elegance of appointment," pointing to "tinted walls, palms and fountains, carved and grilled woodwork and brilliant hangings and rugs" as opulent details "somewhat belying the simplicity of taste for which the 'Chocolate King' is noted." Lowell Thomas, a renowned media personality, quipped that the Hotel Hershey "out-palaces the palaces of the Maharajahs of India."

Nothing short of showstopping, the $2 million property (which has been expanded to 232 guest rooms) retains its old-world elegance and many of its original design features and amenities. The Fountain Lobby, designed to resemble a Spanish courtyard, remains virtually unchanged, from its hand-painted blue sky ceiling, complete with fluffy white clouds, to the gleaming chestnut rails on the balconies and the hand-glazed tiles surrounding the grand sculpted waterworks that is its centerpiece. At least 80 percent of the furniture in this lobby dates from the opening days of the Hotel Hershey.

In the hotel's Circular Dining Room, thirteen colored leaded-glass windows depict flora and fauna native to the local woods and forests.

Another architectural landmark constructed during the Great Building Campaign was the Hershey Theatre, part of a $3 million Community Center project, which has served as a hub of culture and entertainment since 1933. Inspired by Milton Hershey's admiration of the artistic architecture and decorative accents of Italy, the interior's Grand Lobby features graceful arches, polished European lava-rock floors, walls constructed from four different types of marble (both domestic and imported), and a ceiling that is a showpiece itself with its bas-relief sculptures and painted mythical and pastoral images.

Solid brass doors open into an inner foyer with its graceful arched "canopy of gold" dramatically illuminated by wall sconces. Reminiscent of St. Mark's Cathedral in Venice, the intricately designed blue and gold mosaic-tiled detailing

of the ceiling took two German artisans two years of work to complete.

The inside of the main auditorium could be a Byzantine castle, with its towers and elaborate arched and balconied windows. Above the stage stretches a proscenium arch, designed in the image of the Bridge of Sighs in Venice, while an original watercolor-painted fire curtain takes audiences on a dreamy journey along the city's Grand Canal, complete with gondoliers and a view of the Doge's Palace.

"Superlatives are mere whispers to tell you about this theatre," was an early visitor comment recorded in the Hershey Community Archives. "It is worth the admission price just to get a good look at the Hershey Theatre."

In its early days the Hershey Theatre hosted some of the most famous performers of their time, including Roy Rogers, Fanny Brice, and ventriloquist Edgar Bergen. Most performances featured the Hersheyettes, a chorus line of sixteen precision dancing girls modeled on the renowned New York Radio City Music Hall Rockettes. Later the theater expanded its repertoire to include Broadway

When the sun goes down, romantic lighting illuminates the reflecting pool in the Hotel Hershey's formal garden.

Sweet Rides

If it's the timeless beauty of classic cars that gets your motor running, the Antique Automobile Club of America Museum in Hershey showcases every four-wheeled fantasy, from a ruby red 1917 Pierce Arrow Model 38 to sleek, sexy Thunderbirds to ritzy Rolls Royces.

plays and musicals, such as *The King and I,* starring Yul Brynner; *Annie Get Your Gun,* with Mary Martin; *The Heiress,* with Basil Rathbone; and *Medea,* starring Judith Anderson; and classical performers such as Van Cliburn, Anna Moffo, and the Vienna Choir Boys.

A $3 million restoration between 2001 and 2003 brought the Hershey Theatre back to its original opening-night glory. Owned and operated by the M.S. Hershey Foundation, the nonprofit organization created to provide cultural and educational opportunities for the community, the theater remains one of Pennsylvania's foremost performing arts centers, bringing touring Broadway shows, classical music, dance, and a full spectrum of other entertainment to the town that Milton Hershey built.

Unlike the ornate European designs of the Hotel Hershey and Hershey Theatre, the Hershey Lodge is mountain-cabin cozy, trimmed in warm woods, with a four-sided fireplace glowing in the center of the lobby. Originally positioned as a motor lodge when it was built in 1967, twenty-one years after the death of Milton Hershey, the facility has grown in size and status. Renovations in 1997 and 2002 have made it the largest convention resort in Pennsylvania. The lodge hosts everything from corporate events to political gatherings.

Restaurants at the Hershey Lodge range from the kid-pleasing (often chocolate-focused) buffet at Lebbie Lebkicher's to the sports-themed Bears' Den (named after the town's award-winning American Hockey League team) to the upscale casual Forebay (home of the lodge's signature chocolate martinis and chocolate seared diver scallops) and the Hershey Grill (chocolate barbecue-sauced chicken wings and crème brûlée).

The Hershey Lodge has come a long way from its modest motor lodge roots in the late 1960s.

Hershey's Special Dark chocolate crème brûlée

This sugar-crusted, creamy example of end-of-meal elegance was shared by executive chef Bill Justus. It is the signature dessert at the Hershey Grill Restaurant at the Hershey Lodge.

6 ounces **HERSHEY'S SPECIAL DARK** chocolate chips

1 cup milk

1 cup heavy cream

1 teaspoon vanilla

3/4 cup sugar

4 large egg yolks

1. Preheat oven to 350°F. Melt chocolate over a double boiler. In a saucepan, combine milk, cream, vanilla, and 1/2 cup sugar and cook over medium heat until hot, but not boiling.

2. Temper the egg yolks by adding a little of the cream mixture to the eggs to bring the eggs up to the temperature of the hot cream without scrambling the eggs. Then add the rest of the cream. Whisk until smooth. Add the melted chocolate and mix well.

3. Pour the custard batter through a mesh strainer into 6 (4-ounce) ramekins. Set the ramekins in a shallow baking pan and place in the oven. Before closing the oven door, pour enough hot water into the pan to cover the ramekins halfway. Bake for 25 to 30 minutes, then carefully remove from oven. Remove from water bath and cool to room temperature. Refrigerate overnight.

4. To serve, preheat oven to broil and sprinkle each custard with remaining sugar and broil for 30 to 60 seconds or until bubbling. If you prefer, you may caramelize the sugar with a brûlée torch.

Serves 6

Hershey's milk chocolate crème brûlée

This alternative crème brûlée, made with lighter milk chocolate instead of dark, was developed at the Hotel Hershey.

2 1/2 cups heavy cream

1 vanilla bean

8 ounces milk chocolate, chopped

8 egg yolks

2 tablespoons sugar

8 tablespoons sugar, for topping

1. Preheat oven to 300°F. Mix cream and vanilla bean together in a double boiler; heat the mixture for 10 to 15 minutes and stir in the chocolate. Remove the vanilla bean.

2. Whisk egg yolks and 2 tablespoons of sugar together in a mixing bowl. Slowly pour the chocolate cream into the egg mix, continuously whisking.

3. Pour batter into ramekins or custard dishes. Place in a large baking pan and add enough water to come halfway up the sides of the cups. Bake until the custard is set, about 1 hour. Remove from the water bath and cool. Cover and refrigerate.

4. Right before serving, sprinkle 1 tablespoon of sugar on top of each cup and caramelize the top with a brûlée torch or place under the broiler for 30 to 60 seconds until the sugar bubbles.

Serves 8

Hershey's chocolate truffles

Dark, decadent, and unbelievably creamy, these melt-in-your mouth cocoa-dusted confections from the Hershey Lodge are easy to make and impossible to forget. When making truffles, fudge, or any kinds of chocolate candies, don't substitute diet, soft, light, or vegetable oil spreads for regular butter, says Hershey's Kitchens. They may contain too much moisture and cause recipe failure. Speaking of excess moisture, try to pick a cool and dry day for your candy making to keep the chocolate—and the preparation process—smooth.

12 ounces heavy cream

4 tablespoons honey

16 ounces HERSHEY'S SPECIAL DARK chocolate chips

$3^1/_2$ ounces unsalted butter

5 tablespoons HERSHEY'S unsweetened cocoa

1. In a saucepan, stir together cream and honey; bring to a light boil. Remove saucepan from heat and add chocolate chips; cover and let mixture stand for about 2 to 3 minutes. Uncover the mixture and add the butter, stirring until smooth. Allow to cool for at least 30 minutes, then refrigerate for $1^1/_2$ hours.

2. Form chocolate mixture into 16 (1-inch) balls and place on a cookie sheet. In a shallow dish, roll the chocolate balls one at a time in cocoa until balls are completely covered. Place in fluted paper cups.

Makes 16 truffles

warm Hershey's chocolate cakes with white chocolate ice cream
Serve these densely delicious individual cakes from the Hershey Lodge warm with Hershey's White Chocolate Ice Cream and a garnish of fresh berries or other fruits.

6 tablespoons butter

3½ ounces HERSHEY'S SPECIAL DARK chocolate chips

2 whole eggs

2 egg yolks

½ cup sugar

3 tablespoons flour

1. Preheat oven to 350°F. Butter and flour 4 (4-ounce) ramekins and set aside.

2. Melt butter and chocolate together in a double boiler, stirring until smooth.

3. In a medium bowl, whisk together the eggs and egg yolks. Add sugar and whisk until foamy; add flour and stir to combine. Then add butter and chocolate mixture and stir to combine. Pour the batter into prepared molds. Bake the cakes for 8 to 10 minutes or until slightly puffed. Invert the warm cakes onto a serving plate and garnish with a scoop of white chocolate ice cream (recipe follows) and fresh fruit.

Serves 4

Hershey's white chocolate ice cream

2 cups half-and-half

2 cups whipping cream

12 ounces HERSHEY'S Premier White Chips

4 whole eggs

1½ cups sugar

1. Scald half-and-half and cream in double boiler. Add the white chips, reduce heat, and simmer until the chips are melted; remove from heat.

2. Blend eggs in a medium bowl; add sugar and mix until sugar is dissolved. Gradually add in the white chocolate mixture and refrigerate until chilled.

3. Follow the instructions included with your ice-cream maker.

Makes 1 quart

the Hotel Hershey's chocolate cream pie

Layers of smooth, deep chocolate, topped with airy whipped cream and a crown of more chocolate in the form of shavings or Kisses candy. When cooling puddings and pie fillings, lightly press waxed paper or plastic wrap directly onto the surface to prevent a tough "skin" from forming, says the Hershey Company.

2$\frac{1}{2}$ cups milk

1 cup sugar

3 tablespoons flour

5 tablespoons cornstarch

$\frac{1}{2}$ teaspoon salt

3 egg yolks

2 tablespoons butter

2$\frac{1}{2}$ ounces unsweetened baking chocolate

1$\frac{1}{2}$ teaspoons vanilla

9-inch baked pastry shell

shaved chocolate or HERSHEY'S KISSES candies for garnish

1. Heat 1$\frac{1}{2}$ cups milk and sugar in a 1-quart saucepan. Combine remaining 1 cup milk along with flour, cornstarch, salt, and egg yolks. Temper this mixture by adding $\frac{1}{3}$ of the hot milk/sugar mixture to the egg yolk–and-starch mixture. Add the remaining $\frac{2}{3}$ of the milk/sugar mixture. Return all of this mixture to the pot and bring to a boil. Boil and stir for 1 minute, then remove from heat.

2. Add chocolate and stir until melted; immediately stir in vanilla and butter. Pour filling into prepared pie shell. Refrigerate overnight. To serve, garnish with whipped cream and shaved chocolate or unwrapped Hershey's Kisses candies.

Serves 8 servings

Curling Clues

Chocolate curls add instant glamour to desserts and they're supereasy to make. Simply warm a block of chocolate (dark, milk, or white) to room temperature and draw the blade of a vegetable parer over the smooth surface of the bar.

Breads 'n Cheese of Hershey chocolate mousse

Breads 'N Cheese of Hershey is a small bakery/coffee shop owned and operated by Neils and Diane Bilde. The Bildes met when Neils, a chef born in Denmark, came to work at a Danish restaurant near Hershey where Diane also happened to be employed. Breads 'N Cheese had already been established for seven years and had become a well-known downtown Hershey landmark by the time the couple bought it in 1998. The Bildes have built their own reputation—and a loyal local following—with a signature collection of European-style breads and desserts. (Breads 'N Cheese provided catering services to John Travolta and company during the local filming of *Lucky Numbers*, a comedy released in 2000.)

1 pound semisweet chocolate

2 eggs plus 4 egg yolks

2 cups heavy cream

6 tablespoons confectioners' sugar

4 egg whites, whipped to soft peaks

$\frac{1}{2}$ cup (one stick) butter or margarine (optional)

3 cups chocolate cookie crumbs (optional)

1. To make the mousse: Melt chocolate in a double boiler; let cool to lukewarm. Add 2 whole eggs and mix well. Add 4 yolks and mix. Beat the heavy cream on high, mixing in confectioners' sugar, until the cream forms soft peaks. Alternately fold whipped cream and 4 egg whites into chocolate.

2. To make the optional crust: Melt butter. Combine with chocolate crumbs, and line a mold or springform pan with the crust mixture.

3. Pour mousse into mold or springform pan lined with crust. Cover mold or springform pan and refrigerate for several hours before serving.

Serves 12

white chocolate mousse

You can prepare this dessert from the Hotel Hershey up to two days in advance.

8 ounces white chocolate, chopped

1¼ cups whipping cream

2 tablespoons light corn syrup

1. Stir white chocolate, ¼ cup cream, and 2 tablespoons corn syrup in a saucepan over very low heat until chocolate is melted and smooth. Pour into a bowl and allow to cool to lukewarm.

2. Beat 1 cup cream with an electric mixer until the cream forms soft peaks. Fold cream into the white chocolate mixture in 2 batches.

3. Divide mousse among 4 custard cups. Cover and refrigerate until firm, about 4 hours.

Serves 4

Recipe Pinch Hitters

If you don't have the exact form of chocolate called for in a recipe, these substitutions suggested by The Hershey Company will usually do the trick:

· For 1 ounce of baking chocolate, you may substitute 3 tablespoons of unsweetened cocoa plus 1 tablespoon of vegetable shortening (not butter or margarine).

· For 1 cup (a 6-ounce package) of semisweet chocolate chips, you may substitute 2 ounces of unsweetened baking chocolate, 7 tablespoons of sugar, and 2 tablespoons of shortening.

Do not substitute semisweet or milk chocolate for unsweetened baking chocolate in recipes.

A curly-headed cutie is flanked by a Hershey's milk chocolate bar and tin of cocoa on this promotional poster from around 1900.

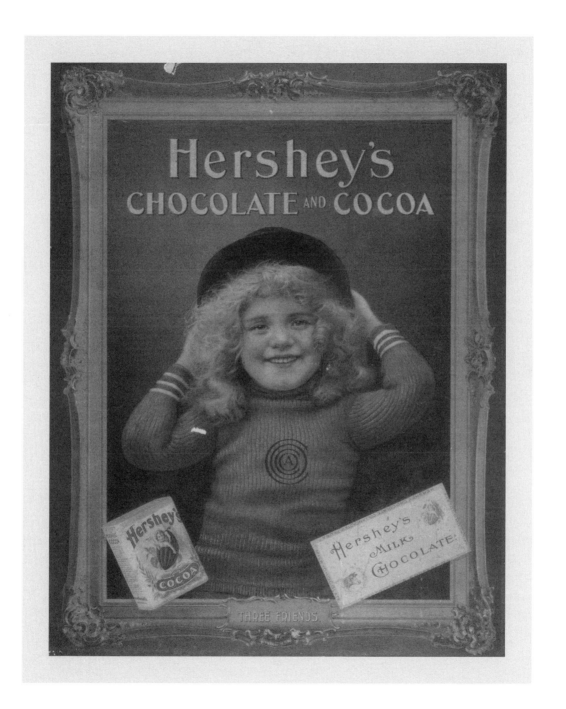

chocolate raspberry truffle torte

Chocolate and raspberry are always an ultra-elegant combination. That's particularly true of this recipe that won home baker Hilary Swanton first place in the "Hershey's Greatest Cocoa Cake Contest" at the 2006 Pennsylvania Farm Show.

Make sure you're using the precise amount of unsweetened cocoa specified in a recipe by lightly packing the cocoa into a measuring cup, then leveling with a spatula.

$2^2/_3$ cups granulated sugar

$1^1/_3$ cups vegetable oil

3 large eggs

$2^2/_3$ cups all-purpose flour

1 cup HERSHEY'S unsweetened cocoa

1 tablespoon plus 1 teaspoon
   baking soda

$1^1/_3$ cups sour milk

1 tablespoon pure vanilla

$1^1/_3$ cups boiling water

3 cups confectioner's sugar

pinch salt

5 tablespoons butter, softened

$^1/_4$ teaspoon pure vanilla

3 to 4 tablespoons Chambord raspberry
   liqueur

12 ounces frozen raspberries, thawed

$^1/_2$ cup water

1 teaspoon lemon juice

$^3/_4$ cup sugar

3 tablespoons cornstarch, heaping

$1^1/_2$ pounds confectioner's sugar

$^1/_2$ cup HERSHEY'S unsweetened cocoa

3 tablespoons butter, softened

$^1/_2$ cup plain vegetable shortening

1 teaspoon pure vanilla

$^1/_2$ to $^3/_4$ cup evaporated milk

1. Preheat oven to 350°F. Grease and flour 4 (9-inch) round pans. In a large bowl, mix together $2^2/_3$ cups granulated sugar, oil, and eggs using an electric mixer. In a separate bowl, sift together flour, 1 cup unsweetened cocoa, and baking soda. Add dry mixture to wet and mix well. Scrape sides of bowl with a spatula and add sour milk, 1 tablespoon vanilla, and boiling water. Mix until combined and pour evenly into prepared pans. Bake for 25 minutes, or until a toothpick inserted in the center comes out clean. Remove from pans and allow to cool completely on wire racks.

2. To make the Chambord buttercream: In a medium bowl, combine 3 cups confectioner's sugar, salt, 5 tablespoons butter, and $^1/_4$ teaspoon vanilla. Add Chambord by the tablespoonful and mix until a spreadable consistency is achieved. Set aside.

3. To make the raspberry filling: In a blender, combine thawed raspberries (and their juice), water, and lemon juice. Puree until all raspberries are liquefied. Add $^3/_4$ cup granulated sugar and cornstarch and puree until both have completely dissolved. Pour mixture into a heavy-bottom saucepan and heat to medium high over stove. Whisk mixture continuously (to prevent lumps) until thickened. Remove from heat and allow to cool completely.

4. To make the chocolate frosting: In a large bowl, sift together 1½ pounds confectioner's sugar and ½ cup cocoa. Add 3 tablespoons butter, shortening, and 1 teaspoon vanilla. Add evaporated milk by the tablespoonful and mix until a spreadable consistency is achieved.

5. To assemble torte, begin with a layer of chocolate cake. Spread top with a thin layer of Chambord buttercream. Spread a thin layer of raspberry filling on top of buttercream. Cover with another cake layer and repeat process two more times. Frost top and sides of cake with chocolate frosting. If desired, garnish with fresh raspberries and/or chocolate curls.

Serves 16

Hershey's chocolate bread pudding

This deeply chocolate dessert from Michael Mignano, executive pastry chef of the Hotel Hershey, needs no embellishment.

1 (16-ounce) package cinnamon raisin bread

3 ounces dark raisins

3 ounces light brown sugar

1 ounce bourbon

zest of 1 orange, finely chopped

4 ounces HERSHEY'S SPECIAL DARK chocolate chips

1½ cups milk

1 teaspoon vanilla extract

¾ cup heavy cream

3 ounces HERSHEY'S EXTRA DARK (60% cacao) chocolate, chopped

4 whole eggs

1. Cut raisin bread slices into 4 sections. Combine raisin bread pieces, raisins, brown sugar, bourbon, orange zest, and chocolate chips. Toss gently and let the mixture marinate overnight in a buttered 13 x 9 x 2-inch glass baking pan.

2. The next day, bring the milk, vanilla extract, and cream to a boil and pour over the chopped dark chocolate; stir to incorporate. Once the chocolate mixture is incorporated and smooth, use a hand whisk to slowly add the eggs to the mixture.

3. Pour the warm mixture over the bread mixture that has been sitting in the baking pan overnight. Let the bread pudding sit for 1 hour at room temperature before baking. Bake at 300°F in a water bath for 1 hour or until pudding is set. Serve warm.

Serves 12

Colossal Candy

The world's largest Hershey's Kiss chocolate, constructed in 2003 to celebrate the introduction of the dark chocolate version of the famous candy, stood 6½ feet tall, measured 6 feet wide, and weighed 6,340 pounds. Made from 10-pound chocolate blocks forty-three layers high "glued" together with molten chocolate, the gargantuan goodie was the equivalent of about 639,636 regular-size Kisses chocolate. If that wasn't eye-catching enough, the giant candy was wrapped in royal purple foil and sported a 3½-foot-long signature plume.

Baking Better Cheesecakes

Don't be intimidated by homemade cheesecake's diva reputation. The test kitchens at Hershey have taken the mystery out of creating this creamy classic:

- Don't overbeat the batter—that causes cracks.

- Cheesecakes continue to bake after they are removed from the oven. To avoid over-baking, take them out while the center is just slightly moist.

- Run the tip of a knife or narrow spatula around the edge of the pan as soon as you take the cake out of the oven so it will pull away from the sides as it cools, making it easier to remove from the pan.

- After the cheesecake is completely cooled, gently loosen the side of the cake from the pan with the tip of a knife while slowly releasing the springform-pan clamp.

- Baked cheesecakes (without garnishes or toppings) freeze when well wrapped in heavy-duty foil or plastic wrap.

chocolate cheesecake
Decorate a plate with Hershey's syrup squiggled from a squeeze bottle and serve this dessert with a dollop of whipped cream and a fresh strawberry or raspberry for a Hotel Hershey–style meal finale.

. . . .

1 cup chocolate wafer cookies, crushed

2 tablespoons sugar

$1/4$ cup butter, melted

24 ounces cream cheese, softened

$3/4$ cup sugar

$1/2$ teaspoon vanilla

$1/2$ teaspoon almond extract

3 eggs

1 cup HERSHEY'S semisweet chocolate chips, melted

1. Combine cookie crumbs, 2 tablespoons sugar, and butter; press onto bottom of a 9-inch springform pan. Bake at 350°F for 10 minutes.

2. Combine cream cheese, $3/4$ cup sugar, vanilla, and almond extract, mixing at medium speed of an electric mixer until well blended. Add eggs one at a time, mixing well after each addition. Blend chocolate chips into batter.

3. Spoon batter into crust and bake at 300°F for 30 to 40 minutes. Loosen cake from rim of pan. Chill at least 4 hours or overnight.

Serves 12

chocolate panna cotta
Translated from the Italian, *panna cotta* simply means "cooked cream." It's light but full of flavor and can make a sophisticated showing in a martini glass, as they serve it at the Hotel Hershey, or it can be made in individual molds.

. . . .

1 pint milk

1 pint heavy cream

2 envelopes unflavored gelatin

4 tablespoons sugar

8-ounce HERSHEY'S milk chocolate bar, chopped

1 teaspoon vanilla

1. Pour milk and cream into a medium saucepan; sprinkle gelatin powder over top. Add sugar and chocolate; whisk over medium-low heat to scald and until gelatin and chocolate are dissolved. Add vanilla and pour through strainer before filling martini glasses.

2. Chill covered for 2 to 3 hours until set, or overnight. Serve with fresh or puréed seasonal fruit of choice.

Serves 6

collier's magic marshmallow profiteroles

Profiteroles, or small cream puffs, are standard at fancy affairs, but they can be time consuming and sometimes temperamental to prepare at home. Hershey Country Club executive chef Michael Collier has streamlined the process with surprising, easy-to-use ingredients.

2 cans Pillsbury crescent dinner rolls

$1/4$ cup sugar

1 teaspoon cinnamon

$1/4$ cup butter or margarine, melted

16 Kraft Jet-Puffed marshmallows

ice cream (optional)

Collier's Fudge Sauce (recipe below)

chopped nuts (optional)

1. Preheat oven to 375°F. Separate crescent-roll dough into 16 triangles.

2. Combine sugar and cinnamon. Dip marshmallows into melted butter or margarine, then roll into cinnamon sugar mixture. Place 1 coated marshmallow into a crescent dough triangle, then completely cover the marshmallow with dough and squeeze edges to ensure the dough is tightly sealed.

3. Dip the bottom of the wrapped marshmallow dough into melted butter and place them butter side down in deep muffin pan cups. Place the muffin pan on a cookie sheet and bake dough for 10 to 15 minutes until golden brown. As the dough pockets bake, the marshmallows melt and leave a hollow, puffed-up center.

4. Once baked, immediately remove the profiteroles from cups. Serve with ice cream and top with warm Collier's Fudge Sauce. Garnish with chopped nuts, if desired.

Makes 16 profiteroles

collier's fudge sauce

5 squares HERSHEY'S unsweetened chocolate

$1/2$ cup butter

3 cups confectioners' sugar

1 can ($14^1/2$ ounces) evaporated milk

$1^1/4$ teaspoons vanilla

1. Melt chocolate and butter in a saucepan on the stovetop over low heat. Remove from heat. Mix in sugar and evaporated milk. Return the pan to the stovetop and bring to a boil over medium heat, stirring constantly. Cook for about 8 minutes, stirring constantly, until the mixture is thickened and creamy.

2. Remove from heat and stir in vanilla. Serve immediately or store for future use. This sauce can be stored for several months. Reheat and serve warm when serving.

Makes 3 cups

flourless chocolate cake

A graduate of the Culinary Institute of America in Hyde Park, New York, and a former pastry cook at the Hotel Hershey, Amber Clay is currently director of the cooking school at the Kitchen Shoppe in Carlisle, Pennsylvania, located less than 35 miles from Hershey. She describes this cake as "soooo delicious and simple to make" and points out that it is particularly good for dessert lovers who can't have any flour in their diet. "I make this moist and delicious cake for my friend who has celiac disease and she loves it!" Clay says.

Made with heavy cream and lots of eggs, this cake, which originated in France, is superrich. A little slice should be enough to satisfy even the most demanding sweet tooth, even without icing. If you wish, serve with a dollop of whipped cream and a few fresh strawberries or raspberries on the side.

1-pound, 4-ounce bar of semisweet chocolate, chopped

6 egg yolks

12 large eggs

1 cup sugar

2 2/3 cups heavy cream

1. Preheat oven to 400°F and prepare 2 (10-inch) round cake pans with cooking spray. Chop chocolate and melt over a double boiler.

2. Combine yolks, eggs, and sugar; whip over a water bath (a pot of warm water kept right below the simmering point) until thick and cooked, at 165°F. Add melted chocolate.

3. Place the chocolate-egg mixture in a mixing bowl and whip until it cools to 60 degrees.

4. In a separate bowl, whip the cream to medium peaks (you'll see the mark of the whip and cream will hold soft peaks that just droop slightly). In two batches, add cream to chocolate-egg mixture. Pour into sprayed pans. Bake in a water bath (place each cake pan in a larger pan; add water to the larger pan until it comes to a level about halfway up the cake pan) for 25 minutes or until crusty and firm to the touch. Serve warm or allow to cool.

Makes 2 cakes; each serves about 12

chocolate lava cakes

These cakes are so soft, moist, and gooey that pastry chef Amber Clay of the Kitchen Shoppe in Carlisle serves them in individual ramekins. When you stick your spoon in—surprise!—out oozes a volcanic flow of molten chocolate. Serve these warm, topped with a scoop of good vanilla ice cream.

8 ounces semisweet chocolate chips

16 tablespoons butter

1½ cups sugar

4 eggs

4 egg yolks

⅔ cup flour

1. Preheat oven to 350°F. Melt chocolate and butter and stir until smooth.

2. With an electric mixer, beat sugar, eggs, and egg yolks until they double in volume and turn light and pale yellow in color. Gradually beat in chocolate-butter mixture and continue to mix until thoroughly blended. Mixture will fall down a little in volume. Turn off mixer and add in flour by hand. Stir just until incorporated.

3. Grease 8 ramekins and divide mixture evenly into ramekins. Place ramekins into a shallow roasting pan. Pour water around the sides of the ramekins, no higher than halfway. Bake for 20 to 25 minutes. Don't overbake!

Serves 8

Big Moment In Kiss-Story

Usually the countdown marking the descent of a huge glittering ball at One Times Square in New York is concluded with a big kiss to welcome in the New Year. In 1990, however, the occasion for celebration wasn't the beginning of a new year but the introduction of a new product, the Hershey's Kiss with almonds. And instead of the traditional glittery ball, a 500-pound gold-wrapped noncandy Kiss clone slowly descended to earth.

white chocolate tiramisu

white chocolate tiramisu Before she went to work for the Commonwealth of Pennsylvania Department of Agriculture, Kyle Nagurny managed the test kitchens of Hershey. She still loves to feature chocolate in many of her homemade desserts.

2 (6-ounce) white chocolate baking bars, broken

1$\frac{1}{2}$ cups heavy or whipping cream

1 package (8 ounces) cream cheese

2 packages (about 3 ounces each) soft, unfilled ladyfingers, split

about $\frac{1}{3}$ cup coffee or chocolate liqueur

unsweetened cocoa powder for garnish

sweetened whipped cream for garnish

1. Place broken chocolate and $\frac{1}{4}$ cup cream in a medium microwave-proof bowl; mircrowave on high for about 1 minute; stir. Microwave for additional 45 to 60 seconds. Stir until chocolate is melted and smooth.

2. In a large bowl beat cream cheese to soften. Gradually beat in melted chocolate, blending well. In a small bowl whip remaining 1$\frac{1}{4}$ cups cream until stiff. Fold into chocolate–cream cheese mixture.

3. Line the bottom and sides of a 9 x 3-inch springform pan with ladyfinger halves, flat sides up. Brush half of liqueur over ladyfingers. Spoon half of white chocolate mixture into ladyfinger-lined pan. Repeat layer of ladyfinger halves, liqueur, and white chocolate mixture. Cover and refrigerate until ready to serve.

4. Just before serving, run a knife around edge of pan to loosen; remove side. Dust top with unsweetened cocoa powder and garnish with sweetened whipped cream.

Serves 8 to 10

premier key lime bars
These tropical-tasting bars took the first place prize for Keystone Stater Jessica Buzzard in the Greatest Cocoa Cookie Contest at the 2006 Pennsylvania Farm Show.

1/4 cup butter, softened

1/4 cup sugar

1 teaspoon grated lime zest

1/8 teaspoon salt

1/8 teaspoon lemon extract

1 cup flour

1 cup macadamia nuts, chopped

1/2 cup white chocolate chips

1/2 cup unsweetened coconut

2/3 cup sugar

3 tablespoons all-purpose flour

3/4 teaspoon baking powder

1/8 teaspoon salt

1/2 cup fresh key lime juice

3 eggs

6 ounces HERSHEY'S Premier White Chips, melted

lime zest for garnish (optional)

1. Preheat oven to 350°F. Place butter, 1/4 cup sugar, 1 teaspoon grated lime zest, 1/8 teaspoon salt, and lemon extract in a medium bowl; beat with a mixer at medium speed until creamy (about 2 minutes). Gradually add 1 cup flour to butter mixture, beating at low speed until mixture resembles course meal. Add nuts, white chips, and coconut.

2. Gently press two-thirds of mixture (about 1 1/3 cups) into bottom of an 8-inch square baking pan; set remaining 2/3 cup flour mixture aside. Bake for 12 minutes or until just beginning to brown.

3. Meanwhile, prepare the filling: Combine 2/3 cup sugar, 3 tablespoons flour, baking powder, and 1/8 teaspoon salt in a medium bowl, stirring with a whisk. Add lime juice and eggs, stirring with a whisk until smooth. Pour mixture over crust. Bake for 12 minutes.

4. Remove pan from oven (do not turn off oven); sprinkle remaining 2/3 cup flour mixture evenly over egg mixture. Bake an additional 8 to 10 minutes or until set. Remove from oven; cool in pan or a wire rack.

5. Melt white chips and drizzle over top in any pattern. Garnish with lime zest, if desired. Cut in desired shape and serve.

Serves 9

brownie cheesecake pie

Funck's Family Restaurant, an easygoing dining spot in the town of Palmyra, just over the border from Hershey, has been known for its fried chicken, Pennsylvania Dutch shoofly pie, and three-layer chocolate cake with lavish peanut butter frosting finish since 1969. They also have a second location at Fort Indiantown Gap in Annville, less than 10 miles northeast of Hershey.

While relatively new to the menu, this gorgeous hunk of fudge striped with creamy cheesecake baked up by the restaurant's pastry chef Barbara Bauch has fast become a favorite among regular diners. You can serve it at room temperature or warm with vanilla ice cream. Store in the refrigerator.

1 (8-ounce) bar cream cheese, softened

3 tablespoons sugar

1 teaspoon vanilla

1 egg

$^3/_4$ cup flour

$^1/_4$ teaspoon baking soda

$^3/_4$ cup sugar

$^1/_3$ cup butter

2 tablespoons water

12 ounces semisweet chocolate chips

1 teaspoon vanilla

2 eggs

$^1/_2$ cup chopped pecan pieces

1 (9-inch) unbaked piecrust

1. Preheat oven to 350°F. To prepare the cheesecake layer: In a medium bowl combine cream cheese, 3 tablespoons sugar, 1 teaspoon vanilla, and 1 egg; beat until smooth. Set aside.

2. For brownie layer: In small bowl, mix together flour and baking soda. In a small saucepan, combine sugar, butter, and water; bring to a boil, then remove from heat. Stir in 1 cup chocolate chips and 1 teaspoon vanilla; stir until chocolate is melted. Cool completely. Stir in 2 eggs, 1 at a time. Gradually stir in flour mixture until smooth. Stir in remaining chocolate chips and nuts.

3. To assemble, spread $^1/_2$ cup of brownie mixture in bottom of an unbaked piecrust. Spoon and spread cream cheese mixture over brownie layer. Top with remaining brownie mixture. Bake for 40 to 50 minutes. Store leftovers in the refrigerator.

Serves 10 to 12

chocolate cloud cake

During her early career in the 1950s through 1969, home economist Alletta M. Schadler, a resident of Lebanon County near Hershey, worked for the local electric company, developing innovative promotions to "encourage folks to purchase and use many electric appliances." Some of these involved coming up with recipes—many of which included Hershey's chocolate products.

Schadler developed this exceptionally delicate, cream-filled and -topped cake to demonstrate the ease and benefits of using an electric knife. "I especially like this dessert because you make it ahead and everybody loves it." Schadler says she prefers whipping up her own cream, but prepared whipped topping works well, too.

8 ounces milk chocolate almond candy

20 large marshmallows

²/₃ cup milk

1¹/₂ cups whipping cream (or whipped topping)

1 (10-inch) baked angel food cake, cooled

1. Melt milk chocolate candy, marshmallows, and milk together on very low heat. Cool to room temperature or colder. Whip cream and fold in the cold chocolate mixture.

2. Split the angel food cake into three layers horizontally and use the frosting between the layers and on the top and sides. Chill in the refrigerator until serving time. The cake should be frosted several hours before serving to give the frosting an opportunity to set. This cake may also be frozen.

Serves 12 to 14

CHEF NOTE: For a deeper chocolate flavor, Schadler substitutes 8 ounces dark chocolate for the milk chocolate.

brownie dessert waffles

To showcase the electric waffle maker, Alletta M. Schadler developed this recipe that gave the waffles themselves a sophisticated new image.

1$\frac{1}{2}$ cups chocolate bits

$\frac{1}{2}$ cup butter

$\frac{3}{4}$ cup milk

1$\frac{1}{2}$ cups sifted cake flour

$\frac{1}{2}$ teaspoon salt

$\frac{1}{2}$ teaspoon baking powder

2 eggs

$\frac{1}{3}$ cup plus 1 tablespoon sugar

$\frac{1}{2}$ cup chopped nuts

1 package (12 ounces) semisweet
    chocolate bits

1 can (14$\frac{1}{2}$ ounces) evaporated milk

1. Melt 1$\frac{1}{2}$ cups chocolate bits and butter in milk, blending thoroughly. Set aside to cool. Sift flour, salt, and baking powder together. Set aside. Beat eggs with mixer until softly piled, then gradually add sugar, beating constantly. Add chocolate mixture, then stir in dry ingredients gradually. Stir in nuts.

2. Meanwhile, make the fudge sauce: Combine 12 ounces semisweet chocolate bits and evaporated milk in a saucepan. Place on low heat until chocolate is melted. This sauce can be reheated. If it becomes too thick, add more evaporated milk, a little at a time.

3. Preheat waffle baker to low setting. Spoon batter onto grids. Close and bake until steaming stops. Remove carefully—the waffles are very tender. Serve warm with ice cream and fudge sauce.

Serves about 10

(V) Hershey bar fondue

Hershey bar fondue You can keep the ingredients for this delicious dip, from an undated booklet called *Hershey's Favorite Recipes,* available all the time (especially if you use canned evaporated milk) to offer a warm welcome to drop-in guests.

....

2 giant (½ pound each) HERSHEY'S
   milk chocolate bars

1 (4-ounce) HERSHEY'S SPECIAL DARK
   bar

¾ cup light cream or evaporated milk

3 tablespoons kirschwasser or
   ½ teaspoon almond extract

1. Break chocolate bars into pieces and combine with cream or evaporated milk in a saucepan or electric fondue pot; stir constantly over very low heat until chocolate is melted and mixture is smooth.

2. Just before serving, add kirsch or almond extract. Serve in fondue pot or heat-resistant bowl on candle warmer; keep warm.

Makes about 2½ cups

Do You Fondue?

The word *fondue* comes from the French word *fondre,* which means "to melt." Fondues are made with cream, half-and-half, or evaporated or condensed milk, chocolate and extracts, liqueurs, or other flavorings. A "plunge," on the other hand, is a thicker dip that gets its less-likely-to-drip stick-to-itiveness from corn syrup or marshmallow crème. Whether you choose to fondue or plunge, be sure to have a wide assortment of dippables on hand. Some suggestions include nut halves; marshmallows; pretzels; cookies; pieces of angel food, sponge, and pound cake or ladyfingers; and strawberries, pineapple chunks, mandarin orange segments, cherries, and apple, pear, peach, or banana slices. (Brush fresh fruit slices with lemon juice to prevent browning; fruit should be well drained.)

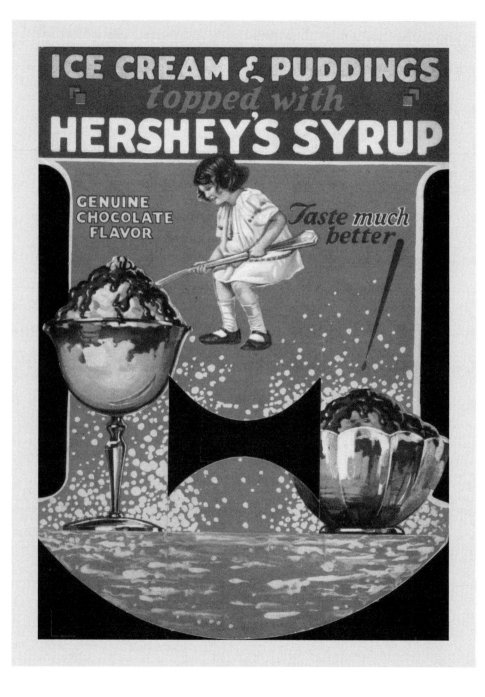

Mount Gretna fondue

Perhaps it was the harmonious combination of ingredients that prompted someone in Hershey's Kitchens to name this dessert dip after a nearby town known for its summer performing arts programs. Whatever the reason, the creamy concoction, introduced in the *Family Favorites Made with Hershey's Baking Chocolate* booklet published in 1975, hits a high note in terms of flavor and sweet-tooth satisfaction.

3½ ounces HERSHEY'S baking chocolate

1¼ cups (14-ounce can) sweetened condensed milk

½ cup marshmallow crème (Fluff or other similar product)

1 tablespoon milk

1½ teaspoons vanilla

1 tablespoon creamy peanut butter (optional)

1. Combine baking chocolate and condensed milk in a saucepan; stir constantly over medium-low heat until chocolate is melted and mixture is smooth. Blend in marshmallow crème and milk.

2. Just before serving, stir in vanilla and peanut butter. Transfer to a fondue pot.

Serves 8

creamy chocolate plunge

This recipe from Hershey's Kitchens mixes up faster than you can say "spear me a strawberry."

1 jar (7 ounces) marshmallow crème

1½ cups Hershey's syrup, HERSHEY'S SPECIAL DARK syrup, or HERSHEY'S WHOPPERS chocolate malt syrup

1. Stir together marshmallow crème and chocolate syrup in medium bowl until well blended. Cover; refrigerate until cold. Store leftover plunge well covered in refrigerator.

Serves about 10

Who could argue with the sentiment expressed on this early placard?

bear-worthy
warm-ups

Bear watching is the number-one sport in Hershey, Pennsylvania. But it isn't the grizzly variety that gets all the attention. It's the hometown hockey team, the Hershey Bears.

Hershey has had hockey fever since 1931, when the first team, which eventually took the name the Hershey B'ars, established its home there. Hockey was a hit from the start. Sell-out crowds cheered on the B'ars as they played teams from Baltimore, Atlantic City, and Philadelphia. When the Eastern Amateur League and New York sportswriters observed that "Hershey B'ars" was too commercial, the name was changed to the Bears.

After three years of taking top honors in the Eastern Amateur League, the Bears graduated to the pros with a bang after winning the 1937–38 National Amateur Championship. Since joining the American Hockey League in 1938, the team brought home the coveted Calder Cup nine times between the 1946–47 and 2005–06 seasons.

Since October 2002, when the Bears first took to the ice at the $65 million Giant Center adjacent to Hersheypark, up to 10,500 fans pack the stands to cheer on their home team during their late-September through mid-April season.

Probably the only thing Hershey sports fans like better than watching their beloved Bears burn up the ice is skating a few rounds on the rink themselves. Both Giant Center and Hersheypark Arena open for public skating at

Many early advertising materials, such as this placard from 1930, promoted Hershey's cocoa and chocolate as good for the whole family.

times throughout the year. For residents and visitors who want to develop their blade prowess for hockey or just for the sheer fun of it, the Hershey Figure Skating Club offers a number of learn-to-skate programs for children and adults. Founded in 1935 and supported in its early years by Milton S. Hershey, the Hershey Figure Skating Club is one of the oldest organizations of its kind in the United States.

(V) hot chocolate

After an afternoon in the stands or on the rink, a cup of something frothy, sweet, and chocolaty is the perfect way to shoo off the shivers. Here's a good one from the test kitchens of Hershey.

1 block (1 ounce) HERSHEY'S
  unsweetened baking chocolate

2 tablespoons hot water

¼ cup sugar

dash of salt

2 cups milk, warmed

¼ teaspoon vanilla

marshmallows or marshmallow crème

1. Place chocolate and water in the top of a double boiler. Melt over simmering water; stir until smooth. Add sugar and salt; blend thoroughly. Gradually add warm milk to chocolate mixture. Heat thoroughly and stir occasionally; add vanilla. Serve hot. Top with marshmallows or marshmallow crème.

Makes about 4 (4-ounce) servings

Better than a Coffee Break

Mary Bonawitz worked in the Hershey Chocolate Factory for several decades beginning in 1934. Her memories of working at the factory were recorded for the Hershey Community Archives. "In the molding room, the chocolate had to be liquid, you know, and it was hot," she recalls. "And then the girls, when we got a break, we'd take our tin cups and go get a little bit of liquid chocolate, dash off to the washroom, and pour some hot water and stir it up. It made a delicious cup of hot chocolate."

Chocolate vs. Cocoa

Although the two terms are often used interchangeably by many people and on many menus, "hot chocolate" is made by melting solid chocolate and mixing it with milk or cream, while unsweetened cocoa powder is the key ingredient in a cup of "hot cocoa."

hot cocoa

(V) **hot cocoa** This is another hot number from Hershey's Kitchens.

½ cup sugar

¼ cup **HERSHEY'S unsweetened cocoa**

dash salt

⅓ cup hot water

4 cups (1 quart) milk

¾ teaspoon vanilla

marshmallows or whipped cream

1. Stir together sugar, cocoa, and salt in a medium saucepan; stir in water. Cook over medium heat; stirring constantly, until mixture comes to a boil. Boil and stir for 2 minutes. Add milk; stirring constantly, heat to serving temperature. Do not boil.

2. Remove from heat; add vanilla. Beat with a whisk until foamy. Pour into cups and top with marshmallows or whipped cream if desired.

Makes 5 (8-ounce) servings

Whip It Good

Whether you're making your hot chocolate beverage from a mix or from scratch, work up a froth with a rotary beater or wire whisk to blend thoroughly and release the full chocolate flavor.

VARIATIONS (add one of the following with the vanilla):

Spiced Cocoa: Add ⅛ each ground cinnamon and ground nutmeg and serve with cinnamon stick, if desired.

Mint Cocoa: Add ½ teaspoon mint extract or 3 tablespoons crushed hard peppermint candy or 2 to 3 tablespoons white crème de menthe; serve with peppermint candy stick, if desired.

Citrus Cocoa: Add ½ teaspoon orange extract or 2 to 3 tablespoons orange liqueur.

Swiss Mocha: Add 2 to 2½ teaspoons powdered instant coffee.

Cocoa au Lait: Instead of whipped cream garnish, top each cup of cocoa with 2 tablespoons softened vanilla ice cream immediately before serving.

Canadian Cocoa: Add ½ teaspoon maple extract.

mulled cocoa cup
Hershey's 1934 *Helps for the Hostess* recipe booklet suggests pairing this spice-enhanced cocoa drink with doughnuts. It's also a body- and soul-warming break for any nippy day.

8 cups milk

1 teaspoon cinnamon

1/2 teaspoon clove

1/4 teaspoon nutmeg

1/2 cup **HERSHEY'S** unsweetened cocoa

1/2 cup sugar

1/2 teaspoon salt

4 cups boiling water

2 teaspoons vanilla or 1 teaspoon
   almond extract

shredded almonds

1. Scald milk with cinnamon, clove, and nutmeg. Mix cocoa, sugar, and salt; add to boiling water. Boil for 5 minutes. Combine milk and water mixtures; add vanilla or almond extract, and beat 2 minutes until frothy. Strain into mugs and sprinkle with nuts. Serve immediately.

Serves 15

Spanish chocolate
Not sure where the exotic name for this beverage from the 1934 *Hershey Helps for the Hostess* booklet comes from, but, if you're a fan of mocha, it will definitely hit home.

2 tablespoons ground coffee

2 cups whole milk

2 tablespoons HERSHEY'S unsweetened
   cocoa

2 tablespoons sugar

pinch of salt

1/2 cup boiling water

2 cups room temperature water

1/2 teaspoon vanilla

1. Scald coffee with milk and strain. Mix cocoa, sugar, salt, and 1/2 cup boiling water. Boil for 4 minutes. Add cocoa mixture to scalded coffee and milk, then add 2 cups water. Beat for 2 minutes with an electric hand mixer to create froth. Stir in vanilla and serve immediately.

Serves 6

white hot chocolate
Mild and mellow, a bedtime cup of this light libation from Hershey's Kitchens ensures sweet dreams.

3 cups half-and-half

$\frac{1}{2}$ cup HERSHEY'S Premier White Chips

1 cinnamon stick

$\frac{1}{8}$ teaspoon ground nutmeg

1 teaspoon vanilla extract

$\frac{1}{4}$ teaspoon almond extract

ground cinnamon for garnish

1. Combine $\frac{1}{2}$ cup half-and-half, white chips, cinnamon stick, and nutmeg in a medium saucepan over low heat. Stir until chips are melted; discard cinnamon stick. Add the remaining $2\frac{1}{2}$ cups half-and-half; stir until heated through.

2. Remove from heat; add vanilla and almond extracts. Pour into mugs. Sprinkle with ground cinnamon, if desired. Serve immediately.

Makes 4 (6-ounce) servings

white peppermint hot chocolate
A dusting of dark cocoa gives a pretty two-tone effect to this mint-sparked nightcap from Hershey's Kitchens.

$3\frac{1}{2}$ cups milk

$1\frac{2}{3}$ cups HERSHEY'S Premier White Chips

$\frac{1}{2}$ teaspoon peppermint extract

HERSHEY'S unsweetened cocoa for garnish

chocolate mint sticks for garnish

1. Heat milk to a simmer in a medium saucepan. Add white chips; whisk until chips are melted and smooth. Stir in peppermint extract.

2. Pour mixture into mugs; sprinkle with unsweetened cocoa and garnish with chocolate mint sticks. Serve immediately.

Makes 4 (8-ounce) servings

chocolate marshmallows

Marshmallows are fun to make at home and add a major wow factor to hot chocolate or cocoa drinks. Hershey's cocoa helps this version from Philadelphia area cookbook author Eileen Talanian's Webzine (www.howthecookiecrumbles.com) add even more pizzazz to these puffs.

½ cup cold water

1 teaspoon pure vanilla

1 teaspoon pure chocolate extract

4 tablespoons (4 packages) unflavored gelatin

½ cup boiling water

1 teaspoon instant espresso powder, or 2 teaspoons instant coffee powder

¾ cup Hershey's unsweetened cocoa

½ cup water

1¼ cups light corn syrup

pinch salt

3 cups granulated sugar

1¼ cups confectioners' sugar whirled in a blender or food processor with ½ cup cocoa and ¼ cup cornstarch, until smooth

1. Line a wide, shallow (9 x 13-inch) baking pan with foil and coat it with nonflavored oil (or use nonstick pan spray). To soften the gelatin, put ½ cup cold water, vanilla, and chocolate extracts in the bowl of an electric mixer, then sprinkle the gelatin over them. Stir to moisten the gelatin, then put the bowl in the mixer stand.
Insert the wire whisk attachment if available, or use a flat paddle or beaters.

2. Make a slurry with the cocoa: Pour ½ cup boiling water in a bowl, add espresso powder or instant coffee, and stir to dissolve. Add the cocoa and stir with a small whisk until it is perfectly smooth. Set aside.

3. Make the syrup: Place the remaining ½ cup water, corn syrup, salt and sugar into the pan, in that order. Insert a candy thermometer into the pan, and bring the mixture to a boil over medium-high heat. Continue boiling until the thermometer reaches 240°F. Immediately remove the pan from the heat. Add the cocoa slurry and turn the mixer on low speed. Slowly pour the syrup down the side of the mixer, increasing the speed as it is added. Be careful not to splatter hot syrup on yourself. Beat the mixture on high speed for 8 to 10 minutes, scraping the bottom of the bowl well after 1 minute. It will first look lumpy, then very liquidy. As it beats, it will become thick and glossy and will increase in volume. When it is beaten to stiff peaks, remove the bowl and spread the mixture into the prepared pan. Smooth the top with a spatula that has been lightly coated with flavorless oil. Let the pan sit out at room temperature, uncovered, for several hours or overnight.

4. Sprinkle a work surface with some of the confectioners' sugar–cocoa mixture. Turn pan upside down over the cocoa-sugar to remove the marshmallows, and then peel the foil carefully away. Cut the marshmallows into desired shapes and coat them with cocoa-sugar mixture. Store in an airtight container.

Makes about 10 dozen 1-inch marshmallows

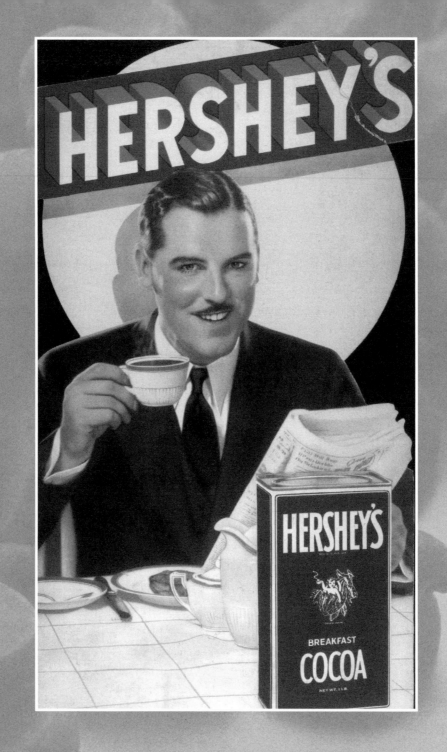

for adults only

Hershey is certainly a family-oriented town, but that doesn't mean all of the sweets served there are designed for kiddie consumption. On the menus of the restaurants and lounges of the Hotel Hershey and Hershey Lodge, you'll find pages of spirited sippers that feature chocolate as a key ingredient.

From masterful martinis to creative coffees to royally rich hot chocolates, these elaborate elixirs are designed for the sophisticated sweet tooth. Whether enjoyed as a prelude to dinner or as drinkable desserts, these liqueur-laced libations are made to linger over.

At various times throughout the year, and particularly during Hershey's annual monthlong Chocolate-Covered February celebration, chefs and sommeliers at the restaurants come together to design upscale appetizer-to-dessert wine and chocolate pairing dinners and palate-surprising tasting workshops. With the growing popularity of artisanal beers, a tasting seminar exploring which brews best complement various chocolate flavor profiles has been added to the activities menu.

Who needs coffee when you can start the day with a warm and bracing cup of Hershey's cocoa? The sophisticated gentleman pictured on this 1934 advertisement has obviously made his choice.

chocolate amore

A little nutty, smooth, and sweet, this Hotel Hershey specialty is the perfect toast to a romantic evening. This cocktail should always be shaken, not stirred, to achieve its light, frothy texture.

1 ounce vodka

½ ounce dark crème de cacao

¼ ounce Frangelico hazelnut liqueur

2 ounces cream

chocolate shavings

1. Pour the ingredients into a shaker filled with ice. Shake vigorously. Strain out the ice as you pour the liquid into a decorated martini glass. Top with chocolate shavings.

Serves 1

the chocolate-covered cherry

For maximum effect, dip a drained maraschino cherry in melted Hershey's milk or dark chocolate, allow the chocolate to set, and place the cherry in the bottom of a chocolate-rimmed martini glass before pouring this cocktail. It's a popular cocktail at the Hershey Lodge.

1¼ ounces UV Red vodka

½ ounce white crème de cacao

1. Pour the ingredients into a glass or silver shaker filled with ice. Stir or shake. Strain out the ice as you pour the liquid into a decorated martini glass with a chocolate-covered cherry at the bottom.

Serves 1

Hershey's chocolate martinis: two variations

Do you like your chocolate dark or light? Whatever your pleasure, you can choose the rich chocolate hue imparted by dark crème de cacao or the pristine clarity of white crème de cacao in these signature cocktails from the Hotel Hershey and Hershey Lodge. For a sweet surprise, drop an unwrapped Hershey's Kiss or Hugs chocolate into the glass before you pour in the liquid.

The Hotel Hershey Martini

1 1/2 ounces Belvedere vodka

3/4 ounce vanilla vodka

3/4 ounce dark crème de cacao

1. Pour the ingredients into a glass or silver shaker filled with ice. Stir or shake. Strain out the ice as you pour the liquid into a decorated martini glass.

Serves 1

The Hershey Lodge Martini

1 ounce vanilla vodka

2 ounces dark or white crème de cacao

1. Pour the ingredients into a glass or silver shaker filled with ice. Stir or shake. Strain out the ice as you pour the liquid into a decorated martini glass with an unwrapped Hershey's Hug at the bottom.

Serves 1

Drink Decor

Give your mixed drinks some decorative panache the Hotel Hershey and Hershey Lodge way by dipping martini glass rims in Hershey's syrup or melted milk or dark chocolate. Immediately dip the chocolate-covered rim in Hershey's hot cocoa mix powder or crushed peanuts, hazelnuts, or candy cane. Or skip the dip in cocoa, nuts, or candy and let the melted chocolate drip down the insides of the glass (or use a squeeze bottle) to create pretty patterns. Place the glasses in the freezer for about 10 minutes or until the designs set. Even if you don't freeze the glass, do make sure to use a chilled one to make a martini.

For a sweet surprise, place an unwrapped Hershey's Kiss or Hug in the bottom of the glass.

the chocolate-covered raspberry martini: two variations
For this summery-tasting cocktail, the Hotel Hershey gets its fruity flavor from Chambord raspberry liqueur, while the version from the Hershey Lodge uses raspberry-infused vodka. Take your pick!

Hotel Hershey Chocolate-Covered Raspberry Martini

1 to 1½ ounces vodka

½ to ¾ ounce Godiva white chocolate liqueur

½ ounce Chambord raspberry liqueur

1. Pour the ingredients into a glass or silver shaker filled with ice. Stir or shake. Strain out the ice as you pour the liquid into a decorated martini glass.

Serves 1

Hershey Lodge Chocolate-Covered Raspberry Martini

1 ounce raspberry vodka

2 ounces white or dark crème de cacao

1. Pour the ingredients into a glass or silver shaker filled with ice. Stir or shake. Strain out the ice as you pour the liquid into a decorated martini glass.

Serves 1

chocolate espresso martini
A coffee bar darling by day, espresso takes on a dazzling new nighttime personality at the Hotel Hershey.

1 ounce vanilla vodka

½ ounce dark chocolate liqueur

1 ounce dark crème de cacao

2 ounces freshly brewed espresso, cooled

1. Place all ingredients in a metal shaker with ice; shake. Strain into a martini glass rimmed with chocolate syrup and cocoa powder.

Serves 1

Hotel Hershey mocha

1¼ ounces Starbucks coffee liqueur

1¼ ounces Bailey's Irish Cream

1 to 2 ounces chocolate milk

One squeeze (about ½ ounce)
   HERSHEY'S syrup

1 cup of ice

1. Pour the ingredients into a glass or silver shaker filled with ice. Stir or shake. Strain out the ice as you pour the liquid into a decorated martini glass.

Serves 1

chocolate cake martini
Chocolate syrup, pound cake . . . this one definitely says dessert. Created by Hershey Lodge beverage manager Karl McCall, this one's a real conversation starter.

1 ounce Absolut Citron vodka

1 ounce Frangelico hazelnut liqueur

1 ounce dark or white crème de cacao

1 ounce HERSHEY'S syrup

2 ounces cream or milk

1 ounce crumbled pound cake

1 cup of ice

1. In a blender, pour all ingredients over ice. Combine until smooth. Pour into a chilled martini glass rimmed with dry hot chocolate mix.

Serves 1

death by chocolate

How sweet it is! This chock-full-of-chocolate cocktail was created by Jason Ferber, manager of the Hotel Hershey Fountain Café.

....

1 ounce vanilla vodka
1/4 ounce Godiva dark chocolate liqueur
1/2 ounce HERSHEY'S syrup
1/4 ounce dark crème de cacao

1. Pour the ingredients into a glass or silver shaker filled with ice. Stir or shake. Strain out the ice as you pour the liquid into a decorated martini glass.

Serves 1

the Hotel Hershey coffee

In the glamorous Circular Dining Room at the Hotel Hershey, this signature after-dinner specialty is served in a clear Irish coffee glass, heaped high with softly whipped cream and gilded with shaved chocolate.

....

3/4 ounce Kahlúa coffee liqueur
3/4 ounce cognac
1/2 ounce HERSHEY'S syrup
8 ounces freshly brewed coffee
whipped cream
shaved chocolate

1. Pour Kahlúa, cognac, and chocolate syrup into coffee. Top with whipped cream and sprinkle with shaved chocolate

Serves 1

For a taste of the unexpected, reserve a seat at one of the special all-chocolate dinners held several times a year in the Hotel Hershey Circular Dining Room.

the Milton Hershey chocolate kiss
Good enough to be named after the town and company's founder, this smooth sipper, from the Circular Dining Room, is kissed with chocolate cream and orange.

3/4 ounce Kahlúa coffee liqueur
3/4 ounce Bailey's Irish Cream
1/4 ounce Grand Marnier orange liqueur
8 ounces freshly brewed coffee
whipped cream
shaved chocolate

1. Pour Kahlúa, Irish Cream, and Grand Marnier into coffee. Top with whipped cream and shaved chocolate.

Serves 1

the Horace Rudy almond delight
L. Horace Rudy was the artist who created the thirteen magnificent stained-glass windows that adorn the Hotel Hershey Circular Dining Room. The nutty flavor is predominantly almond, but there's an undertone of hazelnut for extra richness.

3/4 ounce Amaretto almond liqueur
3/4 ounce Kahlúa coffee liqueur
1/4 ounce Frangelico hazelnut liqueur
8 ounces freshly brewed coffee
whipped cream
shaved chocolate

1. Pour Amaretto, Kahlúa, and Frangelico into coffee. Top with whipped cream and shaved chocolate.

Serves 1

first class lady
A classy combination of coffee, cream, and hazelnut from the menu of the Hotel Hershey.

1 ounce Bailey's Irish Cream

1 ounce Starbucks coffee liqueur

1/4 ounce Frangelico hazelnut liqueur

8 ounces freshly brewed coffee

whipped cream

ground cinnamon

1. Pour Irish Cream, coffee liqueur, and Frangelico into coffee. Top with whipped cream and sprinkle with ground cinnamon.

Serves 1

chocolate escape
If you're going to go chocolate, go all the way with this doubly delicious brew from the Circular Dining Room.

1 ounce each Godiva dark and white chocolate liqueurs

8 ounces freshly brewed coffee

whipped cream

shaved chocolate

1. Pour liqueurs into coffee. Top with whipped cream and shaved chocolate.

Serves 1

spirited hot chocolates

Hot chocolate becomes an adult delight when Stephanie Rupert, assistant restaurant manager of the Fountain Café in the Hotel Hershey, works some mixology magic. Each of these variations starts with 8 ounces of hot chocolate or cocoa (see the "Bear-Worthy Warm-ups" chapter for basic recipes for both) and ends with a generous cap of sweetened whipped cream.

Coco Mo: To 8 ounces hot chocolate add 1¼ ounces Malibu rum. Top with whipped cream.

Caramel Crème: To 8 ounces hot chocolate add 1¼ ounces DeKuyper Buttershots schnapps. Top with whipped cream.

Coconut Almond: To 8 ounces hot chocolate add ¾ ounce coconut rum and ¾ ounce Amaretto almond liqueur. Top with whipped cream.

Raspberry Crème: To 8 ounces hot chocolate add ¾ ounce raspberry vodka and ¾ ounce Amaretto almond liqueur. Top with whipped cream.

Serves 1

Pairing Pointers

Pairing chocolate with wine is more art than science and more personal preference than anything else, but at a Chocolate-Covered February tasting workshop in Hershey, Kyle Nagurny of the Commonwealth of Pennsylvania Department of Agriculture recommended some basic guidelines. Generally, she says, "the lighter the chocolate, the lighter the wine." Dark chocolate goes exceptionally well with port and a berry-flavored merlot, while sweeter reds best complement the lighter, more mellow flavors of milk chocolate. White zinfandel brings out the fresh fruity taste of chocolate-covered strawberries. Drier, fruitier champagnes do poetic justice to white chocolate. Cabernet sauvignon brings out the lushness in bittersweet chocolate. And sparklers such as champagne and spumante are pretty much can't-miss match-ups for any kind of chocolate. To really experience the impact of the pairing, take a sip of wine, then a bite of chocolate, and follow with another sip of wine.

delectable decorations

Catherine Hershey loved roses. When she and Milton moved to their High Point mansion overlooking their town in 1907, she dedicated a garden on the grounds to roses. In 1918, three years after her untimely death, Milton planted another rose garden with an arch entwined with climbing American Beauty roses in loving memory of his wife. In 1937 he planted another three-and-a-half acres with more than 12,000 rosebushes in 700 varieties just south of the Hotel Hershey on Pat's Hill.

On its opening day in June 1937, the Hershey Gardens drew 20,000 visitors. Plantings of annuals, tulips, herbs, and trees have stretched the gardens' horticultural horizons over the years. Theme gardens began to bloom in the late 1970s. The Japanese Garden is a tranquil oasis of water shaded by giant sequoias and dawn redwoods. The Children's Garden is one-and-one-half acres of nearly thirty themed displays; youngsters can learn basic reading skills at the ABC Border and arithmetic on Chocolate Lane!

Still among the most beloved attractions are the roses. Seven thousand painstakingly selected blooms in 275 varieties regally represent the diversity of the species. Many of the original roses that Milton Hershey had transplanted from Catherine's original High Point mansion garden still bloom at Hershey Gardens. In 1938 the American Rose Society honored Milton Hershey by naming a scarlet crimson hybrid tea rose after him. And the 'Hotel Hershey', a light orange red variety, made its debut in 1976. Although no longer commercially available, both types of roses may be seen at Hershey Gardens.

The Hershey Gardens are open from April through October. From April through May the seasonal stars include daffodils, magnolias, flowering cherries, crab apples, dogwoods, flowering plums, and 30,000 tulips. From June through August the roses take center stage accompanied by rhododendrons, azaleas, peonies,

Milton and Catherine Hershey (third and fourth from left) loved to entertain friends at their High Point estate in Hershey, as shown in this circa-1911 photo.

Botanical Boost

For more than thirty years, Hershey Gardens has been applying the clean, ground-up husks from the roasted cacao beans used in the making of chocolate and cocoa as a mulch for its famous roses and other flower beds. The mulch, which is also available for use by home gardeners, has a milk chocolate fragrance.
Note: Hershey's cocoa shell mulch, like all chocolate products, contains theobromine, a naturally occurring stimulant in the cocoa beans, which may be toxic to dogs.

(Facing page) Summer may be the peak season for botanical beauty at Hershey Gardens, but there's plenty to see in spring and fall as well.

herbs, and a variety of annuals, perennials, and shrubs in season. September and October bring their own distinctive beauty when foliage turns crimson and gold and chrysanthemums, late-season roses, ornamental grasses, and annuals offer a spectacular finale.

Not all the color in the gardens is earthbound. The Butterfly House is home to more than 300 North American winged wonders in nearly twenty-five varieties. This attraction is open from mid-April until the end of October, allowing visitors to witness first-hand the entire lifecycle of these colorful insects.

Not everyone has the acreage and energy to plant and maintain thousands of flowers or the resources to raise hundreds of butterflies, but there are some forms of Hershey-style decor that are easy to duplicate at home for weddings and all kinds of other celebrations.

For couples with a passion for chocolate, the Hotel Hershey and Hershey Lodge offer a multitude of ways to express their love. On their Chocolate Wedding Celebration menu, hors d'oeuvres selections include savory chocolate Napoleons, cocoa-dusted diver scallops with braised fennel, and cocoa chili–laced ahi tuna served with a silver spoon. Signature chocolate martinis chill out with a trip through a Hershey's Kiss ice sculpture. A deeply flavored Special Dark chocolate demi-glace blankets an espresso-crusted tenderloin of beef with sour cherry entree. Chocolate butter accompanies the freshly baked rolls. "Hot cocoa rose" or "cacao flower" corsages molded from sugar are accent options for his and hers champagne glasses, the cake knife and spatula, and chocolate sculptures for adorning food stations. Favors may include individual miniature chocolate paintings on easels or Hershey's Kisses candies wrapped in organza bags with beaded ties. Amenities in the bridal suite may include chocolate-scented products from the Spa at the Hotel Hershey. Even the reception menu itself can be printed on chocolate-scented paper.

confectioners' glue This easy-to-make all-purpose "glue" dries strong and hard to keep confection-based crafts at their peak of prettiness for a long time.

4 teaspoons all-natural egg whites
    (meringue powder, such as Just
    Whites)
¼ cup warm water
3 cups confectioners' sugar, sifted

1. Gently stir together egg white powder and water according to directions on the egg white powder package or until completely dissolved. Beat in confectioners' sugar until thick and smooth. Use immediately.

Makes about 3 cups

Hershey's Hugs and Kisses sweetheart roses A single rose says romance, a bunch says true love. These easy-to-make roses from Hershey's Kitchens are perfect for Valentine's or Mother's Day gifts. They're also beautiful displayed in a vase as a party table centerpiece or at each place setting as a favor.

2 HERSHEY'S KISSES chocolates (plain
    or filled) or HUGS chocolates, in pink
    and red foils
confectioners' glue (see recipe above)
florist wire
clear cellophane or plastic wrap
florist tape
artificial leaves (optional)
ribbon

1. For each candy rose, spread confectioners' glue on the bottom of one foil-wrapped chocolate. Firmly press the bottom of another chocolate to it. Insert florist wire into one pointed end of the double chocolate. Wrap 4-inch square of clear cellophane around the double chocolate, twisting cellophane tightly around chocolate.

2. Starting at bottom of rose, wrap florist tape around edges of cellophane, continuing down the full length of wire with tape. Add 1 or 2 artificial leaves, if desired, securing leaves in place with florist tape. Tie two or more candy roses together with a bow.

Makes 1 rose

NOTE: The Hershey Company cautions that this "completed craft is for decorative purposes only and candy should not be eaten."

A Kiss for You

HERSHEY'S SWEET MILK CHOCOLATE KISSES

REG. U.S. PAT. OFF.

Dream Wedding

"I walked up the steps and through the rotating door and was in awe," recalls Angela Fry in her oral history at the Hershey Community Archives about her first glimpse of Founder's Hall as a new high school freshman at the Milton Hershey School in August 1991. "There before me was an open area that was all marble and the most beautiful staircase ever. My mother told me to look up and I saw the great dome, the state flags, and the chandeliers that sparkled like snowflakes. I looked up at my mother and told her, 'I am going to get married here someday.'"

On July 9, 2005, she did. "When it was time, I stood at the top of those winding stairs, took a deep breath, locked arms with my father and brother and went down those marble stairs. Oh how amazing! I lived every girl's dream, I was princess for a day and I fulfilled the statement of a starry-eyed 12-year-old girl."

butterfly Kiss
Imaginations take flight when these fluttery favors created by Hershey's Kitchens light on your table.

- -

2 HERSHEY'S KISSES chocolates per butterfly

butterfly wings (available at craft stores, or make your own wings from construction paper or felt)

pipe cleaner

jiggly eyes

1. Glue 1 pair of butterfly wings to the flat side of one chocolate. Bend a 2-inch piece of pipe cleaner in half and curl both ends for antennae. Glue folded point to top end of same chocolate. Glue second chocolate flat end to flat end with other chocolate, securing the wings and antennae between them. Complete by gluing on jiggly eyes.

   Makes 1 butterfly

   NOTE: The Hershey Company cautions that this "completed craft is for decorative purposes only and candy should not be eaten."

"Hugs and Kisses" wedding favors
A new bride named Shanna first shared this "cute, inexpensive and easy to make" wedding favor idea at www.usabride.com. Choose netting to either match or complement your wedding colors and use a simple ribbon or, like Shanna, choose to have a personalized ribbon made up with the bride and groom's names and dates.

- -

1 HERSHEY KISS candy

1 HERSHEY HUG candy

netting

ribbon

pretty paper for personalized notes

1. Place the wrapped Kiss and Hug candies in a square of netting. Tie off the netting with ribbon, making sure to leave a little extra ribbon—don't make the bow yet.

2. On your computer, make little cards that say, "Hugs & Kisses from the new Mr. & Mrs. . . . " Punch a hole in the top left corner of each card and slip the card onto the ribbon. Tie and fasten the ribbon with a bow.

   Makes 1 favor

heart cookie cutter favors

Use bells, doves, or any other shapes that remind you of romance to make these bridal shower or wedding reception favors. This Hershey-inspired idea, courtesy of Nancy Jaeger www.usabride.com, was the brainstorm of a creative lady named Holly who made them for her best friend's Valentine's season nuptials. Choose your tulle to match the colors of the wedding or other party.

3 HERSHEY'S KISSES candies per favor

medium-size heart-shaped cookie cutters

tulle

ribbon

1. Place the 3 Hershey's Kisses inside the open end of the cookie cutter. Wrap each cutter in tulle and tie with ribbon.

Makes 1 favor

chocolate leaves

Melted chocolate can be a beautiful thing, especially when it is shaped into decorations that add an artistic touch to cakes, cupcakes, or ice cream. This simple trimming trick comes from Hershey's Kitchens.

$\frac{1}{2}$ to 1 cup HERSHEY'S baking chips

20 to 25 medium-size nontoxic leaves with stems, thoroughly washed and dried

1. Melt chips in the top of a double boiler over hot—not boiling—water. Remove from heat; keep pan over warm water.

2. Carefully brush a thin layer (about $\frac{1}{4}$-inch thick) of melted chips on underside of each leaf (coating and leaf will separate more easily if edges are not covered). Place coated leaves on wire rack until firm; chill if necessary. Carefully peel leaf from coating. Store in cool place or refrigerator.

Makes 20 to 25 leaves

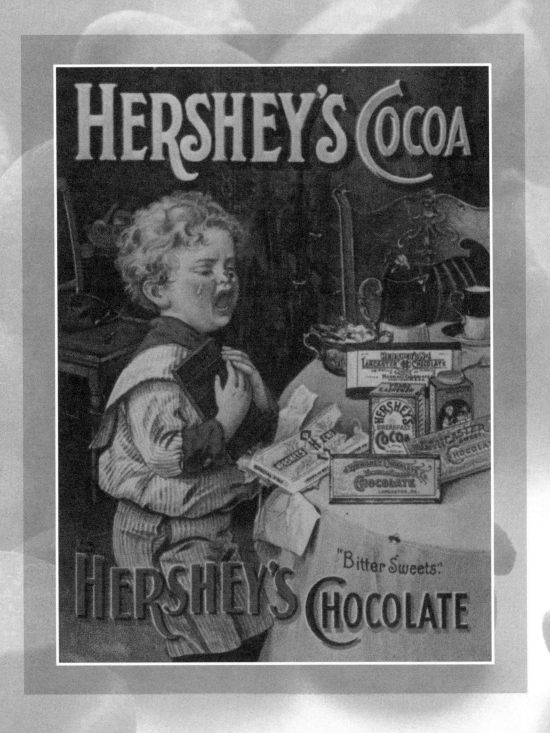

holidays in Hershey

Sweet holiday memories don't always have to come wrapped in chocolate. But in Hershey, Pennsylvania, they very often do.

Chocolate is the catalyst for giggles in the kitchen as family members gather to coat creamy-centered candy eggs for the Easter Bunny to hide, and for nostalgic conversations of Christmases past over cups of foamy chocolate eggnog around the central fireplace at the Hershey Lodge.

It's the inspiration for Hersheypark's more than 50-foot-tall annual "Kissmas" Tree that dances with lights and twinkles with branches of candy-shaped faux foiled foliage. It's the trick-or-treat surprise in a Hershey's Chocolate World Halloween Adventure and a sweet ending to a winter weekend caroling Trolley Tour of the town. It's a heart-shaped Valentine's declaration of love and a family tradition at the Passover dinner.

Some holidays in Hershey aren't on anybody else's calendar. Chocolate has a month-long celebration to itself in which to showcase its multiple personalities and flavor profiles. Annual Chocolate-Covered February festivities include themed dinners (chocolate in every course), brunches, and teas; pairing seminars with wine and beer; dessert-decorating demonstrations; spa packages; gala parades starring Hershey candy characters; and even a hot chocolate and freshly-baked cookie (chocolate chip, of course) welcome for guests checking in at the Hotel Hershey or Hershey Lodge.

"Don't wreck your nerves with tea or coffee, or ruin your stomach with trashy substitutes. Cocoa is a natural food drink, it makes rich blood and strong nerves." That's the message printed on the back of this advertising sales card from around 1895 to 1898.

chocolate peanut butter Easter eggs

Colette McNitt of Events Etc. by the Hershey Pantry catering company says she and her sister-in-law make hundreds of these hand-dipped treats every year at Eastertime just for friends and family members. When dipping the chocolate, Colette uses a skewer or, "if I'm not being picky," a fork. She recommends dipping the centers while the chocolate is just melted and warm for best coverage. If the centers get warm, "dipping can be a pain," she notes, so she keeps the centers in the refrigerator until she is ready to dip and only takes out "as many as I know I can get done in about twenty minutes."

1$\frac{1}{2}$ cups peanut butter

$\frac{1}{2}$ cup butter, softened

8 ounces cream cheese, softened

1 teaspoon vanilla

2 pounds confectioners' sugar

about 3 pounds semisweet or milk
   chocolate for dipping

1. Cream together peanut butter, butter, and cream cheese with vanilla. Mix in confectioners' sugar 1 cup at a time. With hands, form 1 tablespoon of the mixture at a time into egg shapes; place on cookie sheets lined with parchment paper. Refrigerate eggs for at least 2 hours or overnight.

2. Melt chocolate over a double boiler. Dip eggs in melted chocolate; put back on cookie sheets then refrigerate for several hours or overnight to allow chocolate to set up. Keep the candies refrigerated.

Makes about 24 eggs

fudgey chocolate torte for Passover
Passover means no flour or leavening for Jewish families, but ingenious professional and home cooks and bakers have found many ways to develop delicious, holiday-special desserts without them. This one was submitted by Hershey native Jennifer Schwartz to the *Hershey Centennial Cookbook* published by the Hershey-Derry Township Historical Society in 2003.

$1\frac{1}{3}$ **cups butter**

$1\frac{1}{2}$ **cups plus** $\frac{1}{3}$ **cup sugar, divided**

$\frac{2}{3}$ **cup unsweetened cocoa**

5 eggs, separated

2 tablespoons water

1 teaspoon vanilla

1 cup ground blanched almonds

3 tablespoons matzo cake meal

$\frac{1}{2}$ **cup apricot preserves**

$\frac{1}{2}$ **cup sugar**

$\frac{1}{4}$ **cup unsweetened cocoa**

$\frac{1}{2}$ **pint whipping cream**

$\frac{1}{2}$ **teaspoon vanilla**

whole almonds, optional

1. Preheat oven to 350°F. Line bottoms of 2 (9-inch) round baking pans with parchment paper. In a medium saucepan over low heat, melt butter. Add $1\frac{1}{2}$ cups sugar and $\frac{2}{3}$ cup cocoa; stir until well blended. Remove from heat; cool to room temperature.

2. In a large mixing bowl, beat egg yolks until slightly thickened. Gradually add cocoa mixture, beating until well blended. Stir in water and 1 teaspoon vanilla.

3. Stir together ground almonds and cake meal. Stir $\frac{1}{2}$ of mixture into chocolate batter.

4. In a small mixing bowl, beat egg whites until foamy; gradually add $\frac{1}{3}$ cup sugar, beating until stiff peaks form. Fold remaining almond mixture into beaten whites. Gradually add egg white mixture to chocolate batter, folding gently until well blended. Pour into prepared pans; bake for 30 to 35 minutes or until wooden pick inserted in center comes out clean. Cool 10 minutes (cake layers will settle slightly). Remove from pans to wire rack, cool completely, then place one layer on a serving plate.

5. In a small saucepan over low heat, warm apricot preserves; strain and discard fruit bits. Spread melted preserves over top of the plated cake layer; top with remaining layer.

6. To prepare Chocolate Cream Frosting: Stir together $\frac{1}{2}$ cup sugar and $\frac{1}{4}$ cup cocoa in a medium bowl; add cream and $\frac{1}{2}$ teaspoon vanilla and beat until stiff (makes about 2 cups frosting). Spread frosting over top and sides of cake. Refrigerate cake until serving, then garnish with whole almonds.

Serves 12

chocolate-dipped coconut macaroons

The classic Passover chewy treat dives into the deep end of flavor with this recipe from Scharffen Berger, the Berkeley, California, premium chocolate maker acquired by the Hershey Company. You can make the macaroons with matzo cake meal to meet the dietary requirements of the holiday or with flour any time you like.

4 large egg whites

1⅓ cups sugar

½ teaspoon salt

1½ teaspoons vanilla

2½ cups sweetened flaked coconut

¼ cup plus 2 tablespoons matzo cake meal (for Passover) or flour

6 ounces SCHARFFEN BERGER 62% cacao semisweet chocolate

1. In a heavy saucepan, combine egg whites, sugar, salt, vanilla, and coconut. Stir until well combined. Stir in cake meal or flour. Cook the mixture over moderate heat, stirring constantly. The mixture will become thickened and then begin to pull away from the sides of the pan. This will take between 8 and 10 minutes; be careful not to let it burn. Transfer the mixture to a bowl and let it cool to room temperature

2. Preheat oven to 300°F. Line a cookie sheet with parchment or foil. With wet hands, shape 1-teaspoon-sized balls of the dough and place on the cookie sheet. Bake for 20 to 25 minutes until golden brown. Cool on a rack.

3. In a double boiler or over a pan of simmering water, melt semisweet chocolate. For best results the chocolate should be tempered (see "How to Temper Chocolate," page 137). Dip the macaroons one at a time in the melted chocolate and place on a foil-lined baking sheet until the coating hardens.

Makes 30 macaroons

How to Temper Chocolate

Tempering changes the basic crystal structure of chocolate so that it has a crisp snap when broken or bitten and has the luxurious mouth feel we all love. It also protects the chocolate from developing "bloom," the light-colored streaks of cocoa butter that may rise to the surface. (Bloom doesn't affect flavor of chocolate.)

To temper, first chop up the amount of chocolate you plan to temper. Melt all but a few reserved chunks in a double boiler to 100°F. Save a few chunks for later in the process. Then melt all but the few chunks of chocolate in a double boiler to 110°F. Remove from heat; add the reserved chocolate chunks and stir. While stirring, allow the chocolate to cool to 80°F. Reheat the chocolate using a "flash method"—place the container with the chocolate back over the hot water and leave it there for 3 to 5 seconds, turn off the heat, the turn on the heat again for another 3 to 5 seconds. Repeat until the temperature of the chocolate reaches 91°F.

To test if chocolate is tempered, spread a thin layer of it on a plate and cool it. (A fan can speed up the cooling.) When the chocolate on the plate is cool, it should be hard, not sticky, and shiny, not streaked. If this is the case, your chocolate is properly tempered. If it is not, begin the process all over again.

witch's hat chocolate cupcakes

Halloween may be a season known for its spooki-ness, but kids can have all the fun without the fright at the Trick-or-Treat Trail and costume contest for the under-twelve crowd at Hershey's Chocolate World (costumes are encouraged). When the sun goes down, the action gears up during week-end Hersheypark in the Dark off-season openings, when discounted admission gets you on all of the operating rides and entertainment. Spines can't help but tingle as giant roller coasters (Storm Runner is appropriately redubbed Ghost Runner and Soooperdooperlooper becomes SooperBOOperlooper for the occasion) loop and plummet through the night sky. You will need flashlights if you want to follow the evening exploits of the nocturnal residents at ZooAmerica North American Wildlife Park. And Edgar Allen Poe rejoins the living to regale you with readings from his scariest stories during afternoon tea or, if you dare, at midnight. This recipe from Hershey's Kitchens is perfect for Halloween parties.

$^3/_4$ cup (1$^1/_2$ sticks) butter or margarine, softened

1$^2/_3$ cups sugar

3 eggs

1 teaspoon vanilla

2 cups all-purpose flour

$^2/_3$ cup HERSHEY'S unsweetened cocoa

1$^1/_4$ teaspoons baking soda

1 teaspoon salt

$^1/_4$ teaspoon baking powder

1$^1/_3$ cups water

$^1/_2$ cup (1 stick) butter or margarine, softened

1 cup marshmallow crème

1$^1/_4$ cups confectioners' sugar

$^1/_2$ to 1 teaspoon freshly grated orange peel

$^1/_2$ teaspoon vanilla

2 to 3 teaspoons orange juice

red and yellow food coloring (optional)

1. Preheat oven to 350°F. Line 2$^1/_2$-inch muffin cups with paper bake cups. Beat $^3/_4$ cup butter, 1$^2/_3$ cups sugar, eggs, and 1 teaspoon vanilla in large bowl on high speed of a mixer for 3 minutes. Stir together flour, cocoa, baking soda, salt, and baking powder; add alternately with water to butter mixture, beating just until blended. Fill muffin cups $^2/_3$ full with batter. Bake for 20 to 25 minutes or until wooden pick inserted in center comes out clean. Remove from pan to wire rack. Cool completely.

2. Meanwhile, prepare Orange Cream Filling: Beat $^1/_2$ cup butter in a small bowl; gradually beat in marshmallow crème. Add confectioners' sugar, orange peel, and $^1/_2$ teaspoon vanilla, beating until blended. Gradually add orange juice and food coloring, if desired, beating to desired consistency.

3. Cut a 1$^1/_2$-inch cone-shaped piece from center of each cupcake; reserve. Fill each cavity with a scant tablespoon of filling. Place reserved cake pieces on filling, pointed side up. Refrigerate before serving.

Makes 2$^1/_2$ dozen cupcakes

chocolate eggnog

chocolate eggnog From mid-November through December, the town of Hershey gets all decked out for the holiday season with nearly three million lights. Close to a million of those lights sparkle along Hersheypark Christmas Candylane, providing a well-illuminated landing spot for a guest appearance by Santa and his nine live reindeer and other holiday friends. You can catch a reindeer's-eye-view on the roller coasters and other rides that Hersheypark opens up for this special seasonal celebration. Or you can drive through 2 miles of Hershey Sweet Lights, featuring almost 600 colorful displays that light up the night.

After a stroll through Christmas Candylane or a drive through Sweet Lights, many visitors stop in at the Hershey Lodge to sit by the fire and toast the holiday season.

1 ounce Southern Comfort whiskey
1/2 ounce HERSHEY'S syrup
6 ounces prepared eggnog

1. Pour ingredients over ice and shake. Pour into a chilled highball glass.

    Serves 1

chocolate mint dessert

The refreshing combination of mint and chocolate is the perfect complement to a hearty holiday meal. This recipe from the Hershey-Derry Township Historical Society's *Hershey Centennial Cookbook* was submitted by community resident Elaine Wildasin in memory of her son Stephen.

1 cup flour

1 cup sugar

$1/2$ cup (1 stick) butter or margarine, softened

4 eggs

1 (16-ounce) can HERSHEY'S syrup

2 cups confectioners' sugar

$1/2$ cup (1 stick) butter or margarine, softened

2 tablespoons green crème de menthe (or 1 tablespoon water, $1/2$ to $3/4$ teaspoon mint extract, 3 drops green food color)

1 cup HERSHEY'S semisweet chocolate chips

6 tablespoons butter or margarine

1. Preheat oven to 350°F. Grease a 13 x 9 x 2-inch baking pan. Combine flour, sugar, $1/2$ cup butter or margarine, eggs, and syrup in a large bowl; beat until smooth. Pour batter into the prepared pan. Bake for 25 to 30 minutes or until top springs back when touched lightly in center. Cool completely in the pan on a wire rack.

2. Meanwhile, prepare the mint cream center: Combine confectioners' sugar, $1/2$ cup butter, and crème de menthe in a medium bowl; beat until smooth. Spread mint cream on cake. Cover; refrigerate.

3. For chocolate glaze, combine chocolate chips and 6 tablespoons butter in a small saucepan over very low heat. Remove from heat; stir until smooth. Cool slightly. Pour glaze over chilled dessert. Cover; refrigerate at least 1 hour before serving. Store leftovers, covered, in the refrigerator.

Serves 12

CHEF VARIATION: For Chocolate Mint Triangles, cut the dessert into about 12 (3-inch) squares; cut each square diagonally into halves. Makes about 24 triangles.

Hershey's chocolate chocolate chip scones

Melt-in-your-mouth tender, flaky, and chocolaty, these scones from Hotel Hershey executive chef Michael Mignano are special enough to earn a regular spot on your holiday breakfast and brunch tables.

1½ cups cake flour

15 level tablespoons HERSHEY'S SPECIAL DARK cocoa

1¼ tablespoons baking powder

pinch of salt

½ cup sugar

2½ sticks (20 tablespoons) butter, softened

½ cup egg whites

¾ cup buttermilk

4 ounces HERSHEY'S chocolate chips

heavy cream for brushing on top

cinnamon sugar for garnish

1. Combine cake flour, cocoa, baking powder, salt, and sugar in a large bowl. Knead softened butter in with dry ingredients (do not overmix). Add egg whites and buttermilk and incorporate. Stir in chocolate chips.

2. Place dough on a floured surface and roll out 1½ inches thick. Using a cutter of desired size, cut out scones and place on parchment paper. Brush the top of each scone with heavy cream and sprinkle cinnamon sugar on top. Bake at 375°F for 10 to 12 minutes until light brown.

Makes 10 to 12 scones

chocolate-orange swirls

These citrus-kissed chocolate swirls, originally known by their Dutch name of Chocolade-Sinaasappel Krullen, were featured in the 1992 *Hershey Country Club Christmas Cookbook* and *Season's Greetings III*.

2 sticks unsalted butter, softened

1 cup sugar

2 cups flour

2 teaspoons grated orange zest

1 tablespoon unsweetened cocoa

1. Cream butter and sugar, add flour, and beat mixture until it forms a dough. Transfer half of dough into a small bowl; stir zest into one of the dough halves. Stir cocoa powder into the other half.

2. Between two sheets of waxed paper, roll out orange dough into a 12 x 7-inch rectangle and remove the top sheet of paper. Between two more sheets of waxed paper, roll out chocolate dough into an 11 x 6-inch rectangle; discard the top sheet of paper.

3. Invert chocolate dough on the orange dough; discard the top sheet of paper and, using the bottom sheet as a guide and with a long side facing you, roll the doughs together jelly-roll fashion. Wrap the log in the waxed paper and chill it for 45 minutes.

4. After the dough is chilled, shape the log on a lightly floured surface until it measures $13\frac{1}{2}$ inches long; cut it crosswise into $\frac{1}{4}$-inch-thick rounds and arrange rounds 1 inch apart on lightly buttered baking sheets. Bake the cookies in batches in the middle of a preheated 350°F oven for 18 minutes or until they are pale golden. Transfer cookies onto racks and let them cool.

Makes about 50 cookies

chocolate heart-shaped cake with chocolate glaze

Serve this romantic dessert, created by Scharffen Berger, to the love of your life on Valentine's Day (and any day for that matter) and sparks are guaranteed to fly.

9.7 ounces SCHARFFEN BERGER 70% cacao bittersweet chocolate

18 tablespoons unsalted butter

5 eggs, separated

1 to 2 tablespoons brandy

1/3 cup sugar

1/2 cup flour

1/4 teaspoon baking soda

pinch of salt

6 ounces SCHARFFEN BERGER 62% cacao semisweet chocolate

7 fluid ounces heavy cream

1. Preheat oven to 300°F. Grease and line a heart-shaped cake pan or 8-inch round pan (if you don't want a heart shape or would rather cut one out yourself) with parchment paper. Break bittersweet chocolate into pieces and melt, with butter, in a bowl over simmering water. Stir occasionally until melted. Remove from the heat to cool slightly.

2. Whip egg yolks, brandy, and sugar with an electric mixer until thickened and creamy. Fold in the cooled chocolate mixture. Sift flour and baking soda over the top of the egg yolk mixture until all the flour is combined.

3. In a clean bowl with a clean beater, whisk egg whites and salt until they form soft peaks. Gently fold into the chocolate mixture until completely combined, being careful to blend until incorporated and no white streaks remain, but not long enough to deflate. Pour the mixture into the prepared pan and bake for 50 to 60 minutes, until the cake is just firm to the touch. Remove from the oven and allow the cake to cool in the baking pan.

4. To make the glaze: Melt semisweet chocolate with heavy cream in the top of a double boiler over simmering heat. Stir until smooth and melted. Let the glaze cool to room temperature and a soft, spreadable consistency.

5. Turn the cake out of the pan. Lightly spread the glaze over the cake.

Serves 6 to 8

pears in paradise This seductive sweet from the Hershey's Kitchens is so quick to prepare that you won't have to spend more than a few minutes apart from your Valentine.

2 tablespoons HERSHEY'S syrup

2 scoops vanilla ice cream

1 to 2 tablespoons HERSHEY'S classic
   caramel topping

1 canned pear half

$\frac{1}{2}$ teaspoon cinnamon sugar

$\frac{1}{3}$ cup HERSHEY'S syrup

whipped cream

2 teaspoons toasted pecan pieces

1. Pour 2 tablespoons chocolate syrup into bottom of chilled bowl or stemmed dessert glass. Top with ice cream; drizzle with Hershey's classic caramel topping. Place pear half on caramel; sprinkle with cinnamon sugar. Drizzle with additional chocolate syrup. Garnish with whipped cream rosettes and toasted pecans.

Serves 1

CHEF NOTE: To toast nuts, heat oven to 350°F; place pecans in shallow baking pan; bake for 7 to 8 minutes, stirring occasionally, until light brown. Cool completely.

Metric Conversion Tables

APPROXIMATE U.S.–METRIC EQUIVALENTS

LIQUID INGREDIENTS

U.S. MEASURES	METRIC	U.S. MEASURES	METRIC
¼ tsp.	1.23 ml	2 Tbsp.	29.57 ml
½ tsp.	2.36 ml	3 Tbsp.	44.36 ml
¾ tsp.	3.70 ml	¼ cup	59.15 ml
1 tsp.	4.93 ml	½ cup	118.30 ml
1¼ tsp.	6.16 ml	1 cup	236.59 ml
1½ tsp.	7.39 ml	2 cups or 1 pt.	473.18 ml
1¾ tsp.	8.63 ml	3 cups	709.77 ml
2 tsp.	9.86 ml	4 cups or 1 qt.	946.36 ml
1 Tbsp.	14.79 ml	4 qts. or 1 gal.	3.79 lt

DRY INGREDIENTS

U.S. MEASURES		METRIC	U.S. MEASURES	METRIC
17⅗ oz.	1 livre	500 g	2 oz.	60 (56.6) g
16 oz.	1 lb.	454 g	1¾ oz.	50 g
8⅞ oz.		250 g	1 oz.	30 (28.3) g
5¼ oz.		150 g	⅞ oz.	25 g
4½ oz.		125 g	¾ oz.	21 (21.3) g
4 oz.		115 (113.2) g	½ oz.	15 (14.2) g
3½ oz.		100 g	¼ oz.	7 (7.1) g
3 oz.		85 (84.9) g	⅛ oz.	3½ (3.5) g
2⅘ oz.		80 g	1/16 oz.	2 (1.8) g

index